CHINESE COOKERY
Masterclass

CHINESE COOKERY
Masterclass

Willy Mark
Foreword by Kenneth Lo

Macdonald

A QUARTO BOOK

Published by Macdonald & Co (Publishers) Ltd
Maxwell House
Worship Street
London EC2

First published 1984
Copyright © Quarto Publishing Limited
ISBN 0-356-10601-2

British Library Cataloguing in Publication Data
Mark, Willy
Chinese Cookery Masterclass
1. Cookery, Chinese
1. Title
641.3'00951   TX724.5.C5
ISBN 0-356-10601-2

This book was designed and produced by
Quarto Publishing Limited
32 Kingly Court
London W1

Art Editor Jane Willis
Editor Lydia Darbyshire
Editorial Director Christopher Fagg
Photographer Michael Freeman

Quarto would like to extend special thanks to Kenneth Lo for
his invaluable help and advice.

Typeset by Leaper & Gard Ltd, Bristol
Colour origination by Hong Kong Graphic Arts Service Centre,
Hong Kong
Printed by Leefung-Asco Printers Limited, Hong Kong

CONTENTS

FOREWORD

The economic and financial boom which Hong Kong has been enjoying since the early Fifties is probably bigger than any other in recorded history and, despite the prospect of a change in sovereignty in 1997, that boom seems set to continue. The phenomenon is a remarkable one. Looking at the skyline of Hong Kong today, and recalling the barren island it was not so long ago, makes one realize the unprecedented scale of Hong Kong's success.

One side-effect of economic growth has been the tremendous boom in Hong Kong's food trade. At mealtimes, day in day out, the visitor to any of Hong Kong's hundreds of restaurants is likely to find it crammed to capacity and beyond — a situation by no means common in the majority of the world's great cities. A large and prosperous Chinese population of discriminating eaters-out has had a dramatic effect on the standard of cuisine, with the result that Hong Kong can now justifiably be considered as one of the top food and culinary centres in the world.

The character of Hong Kong styles in food is largely influenced by its proximity to Canton (the Chinese province of Guangdong), with its emphasis on seafood — of which Hong Kong enjoys a superabundance. As a great crossroads of the Far East, however, Hong Kong is host to the other schools of Chinese cuisine — Pekingese, Shanghai and Sichuan — as well as Malaysian food, all of which contribute to a kaleidoscopic gastronomic experience.

In all the hustle, bustle and din of the food world of Hong Kong, the name of Willy Mark has achieved special prominence. Officially the food and wine consultant to the Hong Kong Tourist Association, he is also a famous gourmet and the proprietor of two restaurants in Taiwan, where the food is said to be more authentically Chinese than in Hong Kong itself.

On my own visits to Hong Kong, I have been told on many occasions that Willy Mark is *the* man to talk to about food in Hong Kong. The usual demands of crowded schedules having prevented our meeting, I was delighted recently to meet Willy Mark in London — where good Chinese food is much thinner on the ground than in Hong Kong — and to have the opportunity of reading the manuscript of *Chinese Cookery Masterclass*. I was immediately struck by certain points in his book which make it distinctly different from the normal run of Chinese cookbooks published by the dozen in the west these days.

One of the first things that I noticed is that Willy Mark and his chefs employ a very light touch in the use of Chinese flavouring ingredients. This seems to reflect the taste of the top tables of Hong Kong, where preferences have moved away from over-spiced foods. In New York, by contrast, only highly spiced dishes, and restaurants branded Sichuan or Hunan, will do. In Hong

Kong, freshness and savouriness are the keynotes, and the emphasis is on the exquisite and exotic.

Much of this, as I have indicated, is the legacy of the Cantonese school, with its seafood dishes and delicately flavoured shrimp and oyster sauces. But I was also interested to note that Willy Mark has made a point of describing the Chiu Chow and Hakka styles which are quite distinct from that of Canton. The Hakkas are the Chinese 'gypsies' who have been wandering down into south China from the north for over a millenium, especially during the Yuan dynasty at the time of the Mongol Empire. Their style of cooking is characterized by the blending of fresh flavours with those of highly seasoned wind-dried and preserved foods, and the extensive use of animal parts and offal.

Chiu Chow cooking is strongly influenced by the cuisine of the neighbouring province of Fukien (where tea is grown in abundance). The seafood here is consumed to the accompaniment of specially concocted dip-sauces, while small cups of strong tea are drunk as punctuation between courses as the meal progresses.

With these, and his selections from the better known Chinese schools, Willy Mark presents an intriguing picture of the innovations which Hong Kong cooking is bringing to Chinese food as a whole. I think it is not too much to say that in China itself cooking has been fairly stagnant for the past three or four decades, and it is taking a great effort on the part of the Chinese government to restore it even to its past glories, let alone to break new ground. In Hong Kong, on the other hand, with its prosperity and close contacts with the west, a 'sea-change' has been imperceptibly taking place over the last decade or two. Some western approaches have been accepted into Chinese cooking which, being so old and confident and massive, has no qualms in accepting anything it regards as useful and interesting. It seems to me that the innovations of Hong Kong Chinese cooking bear the same relationship to traditional Chinese cuisine as does the Nouvelle Cuisine to traditional French cooking — an approach characterized by smaller, lighter dishes that are exquisite in flavour, texture and presentation. In my view, these changes are all to the good, if only because the traditional recipes of the Chinese banquet can often be over-rich and heavy while traditional 'delicacies' — such as bear's paw, elephant trunks, sea slugs and so on — have become unacceptable to contemporary taste.

With these thoughts and impressions in mind, I can thoroughly recommend the reader to delve directly into the book to make his or her own explorations, which will reveal fresh angles of gastronomic interest not easily to be found in other cookbooks.

Kenneth Lo, 1984

INTRODUCTION

COMBINATION CHIU CHOW STARTERS Freshness of ingredients and elegance of presentation are emphasized in these delicious *hors d'oeuvres* from the Southern School of Chinese cuisine.

'Food and love of beauty are in our natures.' Such a Chinese proverb might be found in a fortune cookie for there are truly hundreds of Chinese proverbs about food. In a *real* Chinese restaurant, of course, you would never find a fortune cookie. That abomination of modern marketing techniques is a commercial triumph of the overseas Chinese, just like *chop-suey* — neither has got anything to do with the reality of ancient Chinese cuisine.

'Chinese cuisine' can be a daunting phrase. It is as comprehensive and overwhelming as any label that is attached to a massive portion of mankind's cultural history. 'Chinese cuisine' is as broad a description as 'western civilization'. No one volume could claim to teach a student the whole of western civilization in a couple of hundred illustrated pages, and this book cannot hope to cover the whole of Chinese cuisine. We can give only a sample, some hints and enough recipes to allow the reader to make a culinary voyage of discovery.

'On a journey do not measure the distance', says another ancient proverb. 'And during a meal do not work out the quantity', it continues, with the poetic sense of balance beloved by the Chinese. Some indications of distance and quantity are needed, however, before a stranger ventures into Chinese cooking.

China is a land of 9½ million square kilometres (almost 4 million square miles), whose 1,000 million inhabitants share a history and cultural traditions that stretch back five thousand years. Thus 'Chinese' cooking is in many ways as meaningless a concept as 'European' cooking. China must be divided up if it is to be conquered in a culinary sense.

There are four major schools of Chinese cookery — Peking, Sichuan, Shanghai and Cantonese. Yet again, as we will see, the labels are very broad, and each of the four major regional cooking styles proudly includes individual regional or local variations and specialities.

A map of China will allow us to look at the four major styles on a geographical basis. Peking is the northern region, a vast expanse stretching from the Yellow Sea (facing Korea in the east) to below the Great Wall of China to the south and Inner Mongolia in the west and north.

Sichuan (or Szechuan in its older, Romanized spelling) is the name given to the cooking styles of the western provinces. These lie to the east and south of Sichuan Province itself, from Hankow in Hupei Province to Yunnan Province, which borders on Burma, Thailand and Vietnam.

Shanghai covers the eastern region. The East China Sea washes the shores of Kiangsu, Chekiang and Fukien Provinces, and receives the waters of the great Yangtze River. Shanghai itself, part of the Yangtze delta, is but one of many urban civilizations that created 'Shanghai cuisine'.

Similarly Canton (now called Guangzhou) is merely the major

MANCHURIA
JILIN
NEI MONGOL
(INNER MONGOLIA)
Tonghua
Shenyang
LIAONING
Peking
GOBI DESERT
Huhhot
PO
HAI
Luda
Yellow R.
Tianjin
Yantai
ORDOS
DESERT
HEBEI
Weihai
GANSU
Shijiazhuang
Qingdao
YELLOW
SEA
Yinchuan
SHANXI
Dezhou
Jinan
NINGXIA
HUIZU
Taiyuan
Fen
Weishan
SHANDONG
Grand
Canal
JIANGSU
Great Wall
Fenyang
He R.
Kaifeng
Yangzhou
EAST
CHINA
SEA
PACIFIC OCEAN
Xining
Zhengzhou
Gaoyou
Pukow
Zhenjiang
Lanzhou
Luoyang
Hongze
Suzhou
Fengxiang
Wei R.
Huai R.
Shanghai
Xi'an
HENAN
Hefei
Nanjing
Hangzhou
SHAANXI
Chao
ANHUI
Tai
Shaoxing
HUBEI
Yangtse R.
Qimen
COOKERY SCHOOLS
BASIN OF SICHUAN
Yangtse
Gorges
Wuhan
Jiujiang
Jinhua
Northern/Peking
Min R.
Jialing R.
SICHUAN
Dongting
LU SHAN
Jingdezhen
ZHEIJIANG
Peking
Chengdu
Tuo R.
Nanchang
Poyang
WUYI
MOUNTAINS
Shandong
Chonqing
Changsha
JIANGXI
FUJIAN
Fuzhou
Eastern/Shanghai
HUNAN
Quanzhou
TAIWAN
Shanghai
GUIZHOU
Hengyang
Longyan
Huaiyang
Renhuai
Dong'an
Xiamen
Suzhe
Guiyang
NAN LING
Zhangzhou
Hangzhou
Xuanwei
Chao'an
Fukien
Kunming
Guilin
Bei
Jiang
Shantou
Dong Jiang
Western/ Sichuan
Dian Chi
Liuzhou
Huizhou
Sichuan
YUNNAN
GUANGXI
ZHUANGZU
Xi
Jiang
HONG KONG
Southern/Canton
Puer
Nanning
(Pearl R.)
Guangzhou (Canton)
Guangzhou (Canton)
GUANGDONG
Dong Jiang
Haikou
Shantou
HAINAN
SOUTH CHINA
SEA

city of the southern Chinese school of cooking, which is found in the provinces bordering the South China Sea, and includes Hainan Island, as well as Hong Kong and Macau. Despite their western trappings, both Hong Kong and Macau are fundamentally Cantonese. Some of their special features will be mentioned later, for it is Hong Kong that has produced the environment in which all schools of Chinese cooking have been able to flourish.

Before considering the different attributes and styles of the four major regional schools of cooking, it is important to look at the historical and cultural factors that link all the schools and unite the whole Chinese nation in its love of food.

When a stranger thinks of Chinese food he thinks of *woks* and chopsticks and of convivial shared meals. But why should the Chinese have developed such a particular style of cooking and eating?

It could be claimed that necessity has certainly been the mother of invention as far as the Chinese are concerned. What we know today as Chinese cuisine is often the ancient response to economic adversities. Another Chinese proverb tells us that 'Whatever will satisfy hunger is good food'.

THIS CULINARY MAP of China gives a vivid impression of the sheer scale and variety of the country, from the harsh continental climate of the north to the subtropical regions of the south. With such a range of climates and geography, it is hard to talk in general terms about Chinese cooking. There are no formal divisions between the great schools of Peking (north), Shanghai (east), Canton (south) or Sichuan (west), but rather shifts of emphasis and perspective.

FOR THE CHINESE, eating is always a shared experience.

The Chinese soon learnt the value of that universal truth, waste not, want not, and for me the classic example of this is the world-famous Peking Duck, which is the basis of an entire meal. Even though it could be afforded only by rich diners in the past, it was still a golden example of Chinese cooks' cost-effectiveness and Chinese diners' culinary common sense.

First, the carved duck skin is eaten. Then the skinned bird is taken back to the kitchen for its meat to become a stir-fried second course. Meanwhile the bones are being cooked with vegetables in a soup. A fourth course might be a dish of scrambled eggs cooked in the fat collected during the original roasting. Then, of course, there is the offal (liver, tongue, etc), and any Chinese cook, from Peking or anywhere, will put aside the feet for other uses. Needless to say, the feathers will already have been sold for non-culinary purposes!

The Chinese *had* to be cost-conscious. The nation has always had to cope with population pressures — even emigration was not a solution — and demand for food always exceeded supply. The Chinese survived in conditions that existed long before Malthus formulated his theories. How?

The answer was to share what little they had in ways that gave each member of a family either a fair share or a shared taste of something special. (However, it must be admitted that even in ancient Chinese communities the women were expected to defer to the males of the family. The head of a fish — the most nutritious part according to ancient beliefs — is still always presented to the head of the household or to the guest of honour so that he may pick out the protein-rich eyes.)

Most of the time a Chinese family might have only a few grams of meat to grace its table. It was socially sensible to shred, dice or mince it, blending it with the more plentiful roots or vegetables so that everyone could share it. If the meat supply was too small even for that, it would be carefully transformed into a flavouring for the vegetables.

That's why chopsticks evolved. Known to have been in existence for over three thousand years, they were the ideal invention for a people forced to eat fragments of food. Hands and fingers were outlawed. Some say that chopsticks were invented so that every member of the family could dip into the food on a table without rising from the floor or chairs. Others suggest that hygiene was a major motive. It is more likely that a frugal diet compelled the Chinese to find a device that would limit any one diner's greed.

Chopsticks proved to be brilliant tools in the fingers of experienced operators. In the kitchen they are perfect whisks, tongs and cleavers of soft foods, for versatility was another virtue encouraged by economic necessity. No Chinese family could afford the battalion of specialized cooking utensils other nations lined up in their kitchens.

And that's how the *wok* developed too. As the modern western world has discovered to its joy, a *wok* is a multi-purpose invention. It can cook anything except roast meat. In experienced hands it can even cook more than one dish at a time, with a metal stand and a lid to cover the double-cooker.

In the north, where fewer inhabitants meant greater access to meat supplies, the Mongolian hot pots or fire pots still encouraged group dining. A family would gather around the cooking pot, dipping the thinly sliced meats into a 'moat' of stock bubbling around a central chimney. Comparable in some ways to western fondue cooking, Mongolian hot pots are one aspect of 'Peking' food.

MONGOLIAN HOTPOT is a Chinese version of the fondue, with everyone dipping into a rich stock.

The deep sense of family is therefore both a cause and effect of Chinese cooking conventions. The Chinese family did not stay together because it prayed together (temple prayers being women's work); it stayed together, as one terrible punster put it, because it played chopsticks together.

Nevertheless there *is* an abiding love of food among all Chinese. It verges on worship. The ways that ingredients are chosen, prepared, cooked and balanced are, effectively, a constant way of 'saying grace', of offering thanks to the gods. The Kitchen God or God of the Hearth is one of the most important to a family. Every

Chinese New Year the Kitchen God returns to heaven to report to the Jade Emperor on the family's behaviour during the year just ended. To ensure that the report is favourable, housewives undertake an enormous spring-cleaning operation. Cracked and damaged crockery or utensils are replaced, and a Chinese kitchen, always scrupulously clean, becomes even more spotless. The Kitchen God must also be given a good meal before he flies off for his annual visit to heaven. Glutinous rice and fruits, horse hay, sugar and bean curd are offered, while the family itself celebrates with a better-than-everyday meal. As with most temple or shrine food offerings, waste is avoided: the humans will consume the offerings once the satisfied God has flown off.

The Kitchen God returns to the family on the fourth day of the New Year, the day when married women are expected to visit their parents, thus giving some housewives at least a break from their own kitchens!

Almost every Chinese dish has superstitious or symbolic attributes. Sometimes the auspicious quality of a dish will come from an ingredient's name. At other times an ingredient's supposed restorative or aphrodisiac qualities are honoured. Other dishes, such as the Mid-Autumn Festival moon cakes, recall historical or mythological events.

A whole library could be filled with books about Chinese culinary symbols. To give just one example associated with New Year dining, consider the purple-black sea moss strands that are a favoured part of every Spring Festival dinner. The Cantonese call it *fat choi* (*choi* being the standard character for every vegetable), and its name is remarkably close to part of the standard New Year greeting of *Kung Hei Fat Choy*, which wishes everyone good fortune and prosperity for the New Year. So *fat choi* is a treasured ingredient.

Above all else the concept of balance is crucial in appreciating — and cooking — Chinese cuisine. The concept, akin to Confucianism's middle way, is the very basis of Chinese society and beliefs. A human can acquire a state of equilibrium only if he or she ensures that the Yin (negative) and Yang (positive) forces are in balance. There are three other pairs of potential lines of tension: cold and hot; empty and full; and outer and inner.

Thus the Chinese believe that 'we are what we eat' and that 'we eat to reinforce'. Food is the best medicine. A well-balanced diet, even among the poorest families, will guarantee good health, for the food itself will contain all the goodness a man needs if it is prepared and cooked properly, eaten in its right season and not allowed to clash with antagonistic foods. If antagonisms have been set up through ignorance, a herbalist will prescribe the appropriate natural cure.

Western dieticians have confirmed the ancient wisdoms of Chinese cooking guides and herbalists' instruction manuals. The most famous cure-all, and an expensive sexual restorative for ageing men, is ginseng, the mermaid-shaped root herb, which is recommended as a treatment for asthma, anaemia, headaches, nausea, rheumatism, heart disease and even indigestion. Indeed, I remember in my home province seeing treasured ginseng roots kept ready by elderly rich men. When they knew they had entered their last days, they would summon their far-off sons and consume the gingseng in soup form. The soup was believed power-

ful enough to keep them alive until their sons arrived back home.

Perhaps, as in many folk cures, a food's efficacy depends on belief rather than actual scientific properties. In China I doubt it. The Chinese have been testing their culinary magic for five thousand years, and they know what works.

Ginger and mint strengthen thin blood. 'Cool' foods calm down hot-blooded youngsters. Bird's nests and petals aid a lady seeking skin perfection. Cold Chinese tea dabbed on the skin prevents wrinkles. Chrysanthemum tea is good for the eyes. Snake bile truly fortifies the over-forties . . . the list of health-giving properties in the pantheon of Chinese recipes is endless.

A stranger need not give up in despair. It is not necessary to know the whole culinary pharmacology. Indeed, there are few Chinese cooks who can remember all the factors, myths and rules surrounding their cuisine. Good cooks rely on their senses and on common sense. For all the marvellous aspects of Chinese culinary folklore are really codified common sense. A Chinese cook seeks to achieve balance, in one dish or in a whole banquet, by satisfying the diner's eyes (presentation), his nose (sequence of aromas) and his palate (taste combinations). Once again we must ascribe such perfectionism to poverty. If a family has a frugal diet it must make the best of it, creating appetizing interest and leisurely enjoyment of a dining experience.

A HONG KONG market vegetable stall offers a colourful abundance of vegetables and fresh spices and herbs, including fresh root ginger, coriander and chives.

COOKING TECHNIQUES

HEAT CONTROL IS the key to successful Chinese cuisine.

Chinese food is to be found all over the world, and the art of the Chinese kitchen has followers and admirers everywhere. Few of those admirers would deny that the uncontested capital of Chinese gastronomy is Hong Kong, which has become a paradise for lovers of the very best in Chinese food.

Chinese food can be divided in the main into four schools — Peking, Sichuan, Shanghai and Cantonese — and in Hong Kong these different schools have in many cases been improved and enhanced by outstanding chefs who have developed superb cooking techniques.

Over the last two decades, I have had the opportunity to get to know these master-cooks on the countless occasions I have dined out in Hong Kong's best Chinese restaurants. Many of them are now my personal friends, and it is because of this that I have been able to persuade them to disclose their secrets — their use of ingredients, cooking techniques, timing. From my conversations and from the practical information I gleaned, I have been able to compile this book of choice recipes from the most distinguished Chinese master-chefs in Hong Kong. I should like to take this opportunity to thank them all for their generosity and cooperation.

The book should give readers the opportunity to learn the art of Chinese cuisine. Most of the recipes in this book are Cantonese, but there are also some dishes from Peking, Sichuan, Shanghai and Chiu Chow. The cooking methods and recipes have all been tested, and the criterion for selection was that the cooking techniques should be comparatively simple. Readers will find that they can proceed in a step-by-step manner, in easy stages. The amount of seasonings may be easily adjusted according to individual taste, and with practice, heat control will become a matter of habit. Your cooking skills should improve rapidly as you practise, and by trial and error you will learn how to adjust the recipes to your taste.

There are many aspects to Chinese cooking, but if you can master certain basic skills and understand the underlying principles, you will soon be able to cook 'real' Chinese food and produce some truly authentic Chinese dishes.

A number of accepted Chinese cooking methods are used continually, and they can be summarized as boiling (slow-simmering and rapid boiling); steaming; stir-frying; shallow frying; deep frying; braising and stewing. The uses of the kitchen knife can be categorized as chopping, cutting, slicing, shredding and mincing.

Remember: heat control is of paramount importance in Chinese cooking. Dishes have to be cooked at just the right temperature for just the right length of time. Generally speaking, you need to use the highest heat for quick steaming and stir-frying; medium heat for braising, poaching and boiling, and low heat for

shallow frying and stewing. For deep frying, the heat should be varied according to the ingredients used and dishes to be produced; it could be high, medium or low and may require variation in the course of the cooking.

SOME COOKING METHODS are swift and spectacular.

Seasonings

There are far too many seasonings to list here, but the most basic category of all are those made from soya beans. All kinds of soy sauce are made from beans, so are bean paste, preserved bean curd and preserved fermented black beans. You will begin to get the authentic Chinese flavour by combining any of the above with garlic, ginger and spring onion. Traditionally, Cantonese chefs enjoy using oyster sauce, and in this book you will see how many of Hong Kong's most famous chefs frequently employ oyster sauce in their recipes.

In my opinion, the following seasonings would be sufficient: sweet soy sauce, soy sauce, oyster sauce, black bean paste, yellow bean paste, sesame oil, rice wine, pepper, sugar, rice vinegar and cornflour. Most ordinary Chinese dishes can be prepared using any of the above in combination with garlic, ginger and spring onions, and with dried orange peel. If your tastes incline you to be even more demanding, you may add fermented black beans, Chu How sauce, shrimp sauce, seafood sauce, Chinese prickly ash, star anise, mandarin peel, cloves, aniseed, fennel, dried chillies and a bottle of brine.

Equipment

To get the best results, you do need the traditional round-bottom Chinese pan, the *wok*. You can use it successfully for any cooking method mentioned so far, especially for stir-frying.

As far as the kind of stove you use is concerned, you will not be able to get such good results with an electric cooker, which does not give the instant heat control or the space between the *wok* and the heat that enables the flame to caress the bottom of the *wok* and spread the heat evenly. Apart from that problem, you

THE CHINESE *batterie de cuisine* is minimal.

can successfully use gas, paraffin or Calor gas for Chinese cooking and get good results with any of them.

Cooking temperatures

The temperature of the cooking oil will also have to be varied according to the ingredients used and the dishes to be produced.

Hot pan with cold oil   Heat the pan until very hot, then add the cold oil. Put in the ingredients before the oil gets really hot and remove the ingredients after deep frying for a short time. This method requires the temperature of the oil to be 80-100°C (175-210°F). When you add the ingredients, there should be no smoke from the oil and no hissing sound. This method is used to prepare good cuts of meat as it helps to retain their natural flavour and preserves the tenderness of the meat.

Hot pan with hot oil   Heat the pan until very hot, then add the oil and heat it to a temperature of 180-220°C (350-425°F). The oil should start to smoke, and it will hiss if you stir it. This method is used to prepare seafood and food that requires a crunchy covering (often battered foods).

Medium heat with hot oil   Heat the pan until very hot, then heat the oil until it reaches a temperature of 110-170°C (225-330°F). A small amount of smoke will begin to come off the surface of the oil. This method is used for frying large pieces of meat, whole fish, chicken or duck.

Stir-frying

The ability to stir-fry is an important part of any Cantonese chef's skill. It is essential to heat the pan over maximum gas or electricity until it is extremely hot. Then add the necessary quantity of oil. When that is hot, add minced or chopped garlic, ginger and spring onion. As the mixture begins to cook, add the other ingredients, stir-fry and turn them to cook everything quickly and evenly. Sprinkle wine and sesame oil at the end to produce a fragrant smell.

Chinese shallow frying

For shallow frying, heat the pan until it is extremely hot and then add oil. Lower the ingredient into the pan and, when it is slightly brown, reduce the heat to a minimum. Use this method to fry fish. It will stop the skin sticking to the pan and ensure an attractive appearance when it is served.

Deep frying

This is a popular technique in Chinese cooking. Strictly speaking, blanching the ingredients in oil can be regarded as deep frying. To deep fry you need, in most cases, adequate heat and hot oil to make the ingredients crunchy and tender. Be careful, however, with ingredients that are coated in batter: keep the temperature somewhat lower, otherwise you will overcook the outside of the food while the inside is still raw. In these cases, it might be better to use the 'soak-frying' method. Heat the oil, add the ingredients and turn off the heat. Let them soak for a while in the hot oil and then take them out. Reheat the oil until it reaches a temperature of 180-220°C (350-425°F) and then deep fry the ingredients for a second time, until done. This method is also known as double deep frying.

Steaming

There are two kinds of steaming. Short steaming, requiring high heat, and long steaming, requiring low heat. Some other Chinese cook books may call long steaming 'double boiling' because the foods are contained in a closed receptacle. In some recipes, those calling for the steaming of a duck, chicken or a large piece of meat for example, you should use the low, medium heat until the ingredients are tender.

Boiling

This is a very simple method of cooking. Simply add water to cook the ingredients, exactly as you would cook soup, rice or porridge. If you want to make a bowl of clear meat soup, you must blanch the meat with boiling water first, and then rinse it under cold water. Heat a bowlful of water in a pan and, when the water is boiling, put the ingredients into it. You should use maximum heat at the start, reducing to medium heat and finally ending with low heat. This kind of soup is delicious once you have mastered the timing and the amount of water to add.

Braising

Cook ingredients over moderate heat with sufficient liquid to cover them. Reduce the liquid to 15 per cent of the original and add seasonings to make a sauce.

Stewing

Add more water or stock and use low heat to cook the ingredients until they are soft and tender. Once the liquid has nearly all evaporated — or reduced to 10-20 per cent — add seasonings, ingredients and flavouring to make the sauce.

Use of knife or cleaver

The ingredients in Chinese cooking are frequently prepared by using a knife or sharp cleaver. Many recipes are prepared by the 'cut-and-cook' method, which requires that equal attention is paid to both the cutting and the cooking. Whether you are preparing ingredients by cutting them into chunky pieces, or by slicing, thick shredding, fine shredding, dicing into cubes or mincing, you must always ensure that everything is of equal size. If you do not, then the quality of the cooking will be affected because of the uneven heating which will result.

There is a Chinese saying: 'If we want to do our jobs properly, we must first sharpen our tools.' To do your kitchen work properly, you need a good sharp cleaver and a heavy chopping-board. Any good quality Chinese chopper will be more than adequate, and a traditional thick chopping-board made of solid wood, 12-15cm (5-6in) thick, is much better than the skimpy modern ones. Many westerners are afraid of using a razor-sharp Chinese kitchen chopper. The secret for beginners is to avoid cutting horizontally. Instead, use your whole hand on the top of the blade, rather than chopping from the handle, and slice carefully into the ingredients at an angle. This is risk-free and easy, thanks to the sharpness of the blade.

Slicing

This is the most usual form of cutting. Slicing meat across the grain makes it more tender when cooked: slices should be little thicker than cardboard.

Meat is sliced across the grain.

The thickness of vegetable slices depends on their texture.

Shredding

Ingredients are cut into thin slices then shredded into fine strips.

Meat is shredded into matchstick-thin strips.

Shredding bamboo shoots.

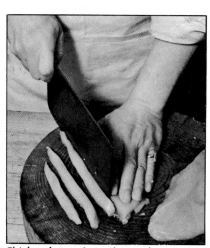

Dicing

Ingredients are cut into coarse strips then diced into small cubes.

Chicken breast is cut into strips.

The strips are cut horizontally into small cubes.

Chopping

The Chinese cleaver is ideal for jointing and chopping fish or fowl into the bite-sized pieces the Chinese love. This sequence illustrates how to joint and chop chicken.

1 Remove the wings.

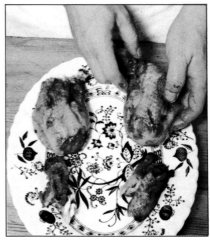

2 Remove the legs and thighs.

3 Cut the breast away from the backbone.

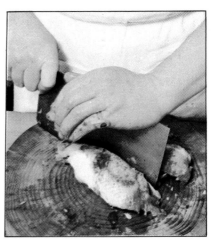

4 Divide the breast in two.

5 Cut each breast into three or four pieces.

6 Cut wings into three pieces and legs into five pieces. Now reassemble the bird neatly.

Pork slices are first shredded.

Chopping becomes progressively finer.

Grinding (mincing)

Grinding is usually done by hand. A mincer can also be used — but some of the flavour will be lost.

Carrots are cut on the diagonal.

Pepper strips are cut into diamond shapes.

Diagonal cutting

This is the usual technique for chopping vegetable such as celery, carrots and courgettes.

Remove the large bone.

Chop the separated ribs into small pieces.

Preparing pork spare ribs

This method of preparation makes the spare ribs easy to eat.

THE CHEFS

NG CHI FUNG

Master of Peking cuisine

Ng Chi Fung is one of the outstanding Peking cuisine chefs in Hong Kong. Born in Chiu Chou, he is now the chef de cuisine of Hong Kong's King Heung Restaurant. He began his career in 1958 when he joined Hou Tak Food Restaurant and learned cooking from the famous northern master cooks known as the Four Aces, who were in charge of the kitchen at that time. Today he, too, is a master of Peking cuisine.

For Ng Chi Fung, experience is the decisive factor in Chinese cooking skills. A sharp eye and quick reflexes are essential — and can be developed only through many years' training.

HO SING

Chef de cuisine of one of the world's top ten restaurants

Ho Sing is the chef de cuisine of Yung Kee, designated by *Fortune* magazine as one of the ten best restaurants in the world. Universally known to Hong Kong eaters-out as 'Seventh Uncle', Mr Ho started to learn to cook in restaurants in Central District, Hong Kong, at the age of nine. During the World War II, he ran his own restaurant in Canton but returned to Hong Kong after the war and has been in his present position as the Kitchen Master since 1970. Like all first-rate chefs, Mr Ho pays special attention to selecting the freshest ingredients and tailoring menus to the individual occasion. The element of harmony is of the greatest importance in Mr Ho's approach, whether it is the aesthetic harmony of tastes, flavors and aromas or the practical coordination of prepared ingredients and cooking temperatures.

LEUNG KING

Hong Kong's Number One chef

Mr Leung King has reigned supreme as the premier chef of Hong Kong for longer than most people can remember. Now 72, he has been working in the kitchen for 60 years. When he was the chief chef of Lok Yu Tea House, knowledgeable customers insisted that their dishes were prepared personally by him. He is particularly famous for preparing the game recipes and 'Phoenix City Style' cuisine, which many people think of as the cream of Cantonese cooking. I have been fortunate enough to know 'Uncle King' for many years, and his advice has been invaluable in preparing this book.

CHAN WING YUEN
Master of Sichuan cuisine

Not many chefs working in Sichuan restaurants are themselves originally from the province itself. Chan Wing Yuen is one of the exceptions. Born in Chung King City, Sichuan, he is now the chef de cuisine at the Cleveland Sichuan Restaurant. From the age of 16 he started cooking under his father's direction, and he later worked with many famous chefs to improve his techniques.

Chan Wing Yuen has tried to preserve the style of traditional Sichuan Cuisine while at the same time exploring the possibility of using new ingredients. He points out that many people identify Sichuan cuisine only with hot spicy food — but in fact, the balance of seasonings in the preparation of Sichuan cuisine is very complex. The characteristic Sichuan seasonings and methods should combine with mellow color, fragrant smell and taste to make a deliciously balanced ensemble.

HO PAK
King of Young Pigeon

Ho Pak is the principal chef of the Lung Wah Hotel — famous throughout the world for its succulent roast pigeon dishes. Mr Ho did not begin to learn cooking until he was 37, when he started at the Lung Wah. His most famous recipes are young pigeon in soy sauce and young pigeon baked in salt.

LEE BUN
Master of Shark's Fin cookery

Lee Bun is the chief chef of Sin Tung Lok Shark's Fins Restaurant at the Harbour City. Now 36, he joined the profession at the age of 16. In 20 years of cooking experience he has studied under famous masters of cooking, and specializes in cooking shark's fin, abalone, sea food and game. Mr Lee is famous for the care he brings to selecting ingredients for freshness and quality.

LEUNG KUNG
Versatile master of Chinese cuisine

Leung Kung is the principal chef for Chinese cuisine at the Food Street chain of restaurants. At 52, he has 37 years of cooking experience. Having undergone a traditional training under famous cooking masters, he believes that the mastery of the Chinese chef is expressed in an effortless, instinctive control, born of long experience, in blending ingredients, seasoning and cooking temperature to produce food at its very best. Mr Leung defines his own approach to cooking as 'open-mindedness and objectivity'. The range of cuisines offered by the Food Street chain is ample evidence of the breadth of his interests and his willingness to learn.

SOUTHERN SCHOOL

GEESE FLOCKS on a southern farm.

It is Cantonese cooking that most people think of when they think of Chinese food. Waves of emigration from the city and countryside of Guangdong, formerly known as Kwongtung, Province from the mid-nineteenth century onwards established the Cantonese as the major portion of the world's overseas Chinese population. The Fukienese emigrated to the Philippines, the Hoklo to Singapore, but the Cantonese went further afield in search of their family fortunes.

They left China, for London or Hawaii, for the goldfields of Australia, California or Canada, or for wherever a boat could take them, for economic reasons. Although Guangdong Province was naturally fairly fertile and favoured with fish and cereals, the peasant's life in some less blessed areas was hard. The Cantonese emigrants worked hard and they saved hard to send money home to support their families and add an ancestral home to their clan villages. When the goldfields ran out or when the railway tracks reached the end of their lines, the Cantonese workers stayed on. Social and economic pressures often restricted them to three activities in which they could be independent: laundries, market gardens and restaurants.

All three interests echoed Cantonese ways of life. Cleanliness is indeed next to godliness for a Cantonese mother, and freshness is a fetish with some Cantonese cooks, who will go to the markets twice-daily to ensure that the family food is glisteningly fresh. Climatic reasons largely account for that health-consciousness. Guangdong and the neighbouring province of Guangxi are subtropical, with long spells of humidity. Before refrigerators were available, storing food was not feasible, and the alternative of preserving ingredients rarely appealed to Cantonese tastes.

The Cantonese adherence to ancient Taoist ideas about the scientific and systematic uses of food further accounts for that passion for freshness. The Cantonese believe that, on the whole, ingredients should be changed as little as possible during cooking. Cooking methods should therefore be as simple, straightforward and brief as possible. Vegetables are stir-fried and fish steamed to keep them as near to their natural state as possible, consistent with the dishes being made appetizing. In common with other Chinese however, the Cantonese do not eat much that is raw; steak tartare, pink lamb and *sashimi* have taken a long time to find appreciative palates in Hong Kong.

If raw food is unacceptable so is food that has been over-cooked. 'Double boiled' soups and 'long simmered' dishes are exceptions in the Cantonese kitchen: food should be braised or stewed briefly, for only a few minutes, which, of course, brings this ancient Chinese style of cooking into line with modern theories of nutrition.

After cleanliness and freshness, the Taoist-influenced Cantonese placed great faith in vegetables. Vegetable cultivation was a major activity between the twice-annual rice harvests, the vegetable plots filling the gaps in a family's or village's plots of land. Even now, the small territory of Hong Kong, a land-hungry enclave, manages to produce a large proportion of its own fresh vegetables. A Hong Kong Cantonese cook may depend on China for running water, pork, chickens, ducks and most of his rice, but he can find his staple vegetables in local markets.

In line with Taoist beliefs, the Cantonese old wives' tales advise which vegetable to eat or cook with which meat or fish, when and why. Each vegetable has its season and its special attributes. Wrong contrasts are reputed to cause digestive disasters. Excesses of any particular vegetable or root have dire consequences, from cramps while you are swimming to insomnia.

Raised on detailed analyses of food, a Cantonese child nearly always became a knowledgeable gourmet, for his region's cuisine has great scope. Guangdong Province has a kindly climate, plenty of water and fertile ground. Versatility was encouraged. The Cantonese consequently have been more ingenious, innovative and inventive when it comes to food than any other Chinese. As we have seen, economic necessity compelled the Cantonese to be catholic in their tastes, but whether that or their natural love of dabbling in the kitchen arts came first is debatable. All we may say for sure is that Cantonese cooks are the best.

An old Chinese saying claims that an ideal life would be achieved if one were born in Suzhou (famed for its beautiful women), got dressed in Hangzhou (famed for fine silks), died in Luzhou (where the best coffin wood is found) but ate in Guangzhou (Canton). There is truth in this poetic balance.

CANTONESE CHEFS take pride in presenting food beautifully.

The inhabitants of Guangdong and Guangxi were independent characters. Only partially absorbed into the Han empire during the Chin dynasty (a little over 2,000 years ago), the Cantonese, like other southerners, have kept their own dialect and culinary traditions. They are particularly proud of their culinary imaginativeness. A Cantonese saying asserts that anything that walks, swims, crawls or flies with its back to Heaven is edible.

Adaptability is another feature of the Cantonese. Two of the region's best-known dishes illustrate this. Sweet-and-sour pork and *chop-suey* — many a Westerner's idea of typical Chinese food (together with fried rice) — are recent Cantonese inventions. Designed to satisfy the tastes of 'red-haired barbarians', the dishes are, ironically, 'typically' Cantonese.

The taste contrasts in sweet-and-sour pork are a favourite Cantonese cooking ploy, the use of one flavour highlighting another. However, the dish was supposedly invented in Guangzhou (Canton city), for centuries a port open to foreign influences ever since Arab traders arrived fifteen centuries ago.

The Mandarins from northern China were also considered foreigners. The Hans brought their own house-chefs when they set up offices in the south, and that led to the further broadening of Cantonese recipes and the development of skilled Cantonese 'Pekinese' cooks. When Europeans settled in Guangzhou to pursue their own trade interests directly, rather than through Arab middlemen, outside influences further expanded Cantonese cuisine. First the Portuguese, then every other nation had its colony of traders dealing in silk, tea, porcelain, spices and other products. Most of them loved sweet-and-sour dishes.

Meanwhile, in nineteenth-century Guangzhou, the development of a true Cantonese cuisine was being pushed to a new peak by the city's wealthy class. Salt merchants and the tycoons of the thirteen *hongs* (agents) of foreign traders encouraged their cooks to outrival each other, and, as in Imperial Peking, an age of ostentatiously grand dining dawned.

The Cantonese had always believed in eating anything. Their love of frog legs, turtles, dogs, snakes and many kinds of exotic species was greater than that of other Chinese. Wealth allowed the merchant class to discover new, costly ingredients, or to persevere until their cooks had worked out the proper cooking methods for each ingredient. The expensive shark's fin and bird's nest dishes were perfected by the Cantonese and their cousins, the Chiu Chow people.

FRESH BEAN CURD on a Hong Kong market stall.

Before we turn to Chiu Chow territory we must not forget Guangdong Province's greatest contribution to Chinese cuisine — *dimsum*, those tasty little snacks that are ideal for taking with tea and were, indeed, virtually invented as a tea-shop cuisine. The Chinese characters of the word indicate their purpose — 'touch the heart' — and show that *dimsum* are a Cantonese passion.

There are possibly 2,000 different varieties of *dimsum*, for the Cantonese prefer to have a number of small meals each day rather than a few large ones (just as Filipinos take *merienda* snacks all day long). A Cantonese day starts with morning tea (*yum cha*) and a *dimsum* breakfast. The delicate *dimsum* concoctions are generally steamed by well-paid specialist cooks who are a law unto themselves. Rarely made at home, *dimsum* are a fine excuse for eating out — from dawn to dusk in Hong Kong — and the average *dimsum* restaurant will offer at least sixty varieties, depending on the season and market supplies.

The tea-drinking habits of the Chiu Chow illustrate how different they are from the Cantonese. The Chiu Chow people originate from the area around the seaport of Swatow in the east of Guangdong Province. Being so close to the Fukien border, it is not surprising that strong Fukienese influences are found in Chiu Chow cuisine. The special Chiu Chow tea is a very good example. Probably China's strongest, bitterest tea, the 'Iron Buddha' tea from Fukien is sipped out of thimble-sized cups. Two cups for each diner before a meal prepare the digestive juices for the heartiness of Chiu Chow food; two cups each after a meal settle the digestion.

As Chiu Chow is by the sea, seafood features largely on the menu, with special recipes for fish, prawn, crabs, oysters and clams. Chiu Chow people put great emphasis on sauces and flavourings to accompany their food, using garlic-vinegar sauce as a dip for spicy goose, while broad bean paste accompanies fish and tangerine jam flatters steamed lobsters.

The third major subdivision within Cantonese cuisine is that of the Hakka people. They are of northern Chinese origin who, having migrated south, mainly settled in Guangdong and Fukien, acquiring the name Hakka (or 'guest family') from the southerners. The thirteenth-century Mongol invasion is said to have prompted their wandering. Because they had been wandering for so long, their cuisine had become one that featured simple dishes and preserved ingredients.

Hakka cuisine is basically poorer than those of the Cantonese

and Chiu Chow. It is considered to have the strongest flavours of all, and it includes dishes like salt-roasted chicken, stuffed bean curd, fried beef balls with vegetables and other simple recipes. It is similar to the others in its preference for contrasted, natural flavours and its willingness to cook anything and any part of a carcass. That was a natural trait for a wandering people, and one that is shared by the 'sea gypsies' of the east coast, such as the Hoklo. As in their food and that of the Chiu Chow, Fukienese influences merge with those of Guangdong.

Hong Kong is the birthplace of the third stage of the development of Cantonese cuisine. Lobster salad, Chinese vegetables in Portuguese sauce, baked stuffed conch and the various 'sizzling' styled Chinese dishes are typical examples of the creativity of Hong Kong chefs in presenting Chinese food in western culinary styles. Even restaurant service styles have been westernized, and an almost French-style elegance is now common in top restaurants. Soups will be ladled out, main dishes spooned out individually and all dishes presented on silver platters. However, Hong Kong restaurants have never tried to introduce fortune cookies. The proximity to Guangzhou has kept Hong Kong Cantonese food authentic, while the knowledge of western culinary practices has inspired Hong Kong Cantonese cooks to experiment in ways that have added a new finesse to their classic repertoires.

GUANGDONG PROVINCE has an agreeable climate, fertile soil and plenty of water, which make it ideal for farming. Here a Hakka woman, in traditional dress, tends cattle.

PEPPERY SHRIMPS

600g (1½lb) shrimps	1 tsp chopped garlic
450ml (16floz/2 cups) peanut oil	1 tsp minced red chilli
2 tsp salt	1 tsp Chinese yellow wine
½ tsp sugar	

Trim and devein the shrimps but leave the shells on. Pat them dry and set aside.

Heat the peanut oil in a pan and add the shrimps to fry for 2 minutes. Turn off the heat and let them sit in the oil for another 2 minutes. Drain and set aside.

Reheat the pan and add the salt, stirring over a low heat until it is slightly browned. Transfer the salt to a saucer and mix with ½ tsp sugar. Set aside.

Heat 1 tbsp oil in pan. Add the garlic and chilli and return the shrimps. Stir-fry them over a high heat for 1 minute and add the Chinese yellow wine, stirring for 20 seconds. Sprinkle the salt and sugar mixture over the shrimps, stir-fry for a further 30 seconds and serve.

This is a deliciously hot and spicy Cantonese dish — which is also the restaurant chef's trade secret to disguise shrimps no longer in prime condition!

CREAM OF SWEET CORN AND FISH SOUP

250g (9oz) fillet of cod or any white fish	450ml (16floz/2 cups) chicken stock
	1 tin cream of sweet corn (225g/ 8oz)
Seasoning	1 tbsp cornflour
1 tsp salt	2 eggs
½ tsp sesame oil	1 tbsp chopped coriander
½ tsp pepper	
1 tsp cornflour	**Garnish**
225ml (8floz/1 cup) water	2 tbsp finely chopped ham

Dice the fillet of fish into small pieces and mix well with the seasoning ingredients. Set aside.

Boil the water and add the seasoned fish, removing the fish from the water when it starts to boil again. Set aside.

Heat the chicken stock in a pan and stir in the cream of sweet corn. Mix the cornflour with 1 tbsp of water and add to the sweet corn mixture. Beat the eggs and add them to the mixture with the diced fish and chopped coriander.

Garnish with finely chopped ham.

夏令小炒

STIR-FRIED SHRIMP AND CHICKEN WITH ONION, CUCUMBER AND FRESH MUSHROOMS

250-300g (9-11oz) chicken breasts
3 tsp cornflour
3 tsp salt
$\frac{1}{4}$ tsp pepper
1 tsp sesame oil
300g (11oz) shrimps, shelled and
    deveined
1 egg white
1 medium onion
300g (11oz) cucumber
200g (7oz) fresh button
    mushrooms
450ml (16floz/2 cups) boiling
    water (for blanching

    mushrooms)
450ml (16floz/2 cups) peanut oil
2 tsp chopped ginger
2 tsp chopped garlic

Sauce
1 tbsp oyster sauce
1 tbsp light soy sauce
1 tsp dark soy sauce
1 tsp sesame oil
1 tsp sugar
8 tbsp chicken stock
1 tbsp cornflour
1 tsp Chinese yellow wine

Cut the chicken breasts into slices. Marinate the slices in a mixture of 1 tsp cornflour, $\frac{1}{2}$ tsp salt, $\frac{1}{4}$ tsp pepper and 1 tsp sesame oil. Set to one side.

Clean the shrimps, pat them dry and mix them with 1 egg white, 2 tsp cornflour and $\frac{1}{2}$ tsp salt. Refrigerate them for 1 hour.

Cut the onion into wedges and separate the pieces, and cut the cucumber into 1cm ($\frac{1}{2}$in) slices.

Halve the fresh mushrooms and blanch them in boiling water with 2 tsp salt added for $1\frac{1}{2}$ minutes. Remove from the water and drain well.

Heat the oil in a pan until hot and add the shrimps, stirring to separate them. As soon as their colour changes, take them out of the pan. Drain and set aside.

Turn off the heat and add the chicken, again stirring to separate. Remove when the colour changes (in $1\frac{1}{2}$ minutes). Drain and set aside.

Heat 1 tbsp oil in the pan. Add the onion, stir and cook until soft. Transfer to a plate.

Heat 1 tbsp oil in the pan, adding 1 tsp ginger and 1 tsp garlic. When the aroma arises, add the fresh mushrooms, stir and cook for 30 seconds. Add the cucumber slices, stir and cook for 30 seconds. Transfer to a plate.

Heat 2 tbsp oil in the pan. Add the remaining chopped ginger and garlic and, when the aroma arises, add the shrimps and chicken. Stir and cook for 1 minute over a medium heat. Return the onion, cucumber and mushrooms to the pan. Mix the sauce ingredients and add to the pan, stirring rapidly over a very high heat for 45 seconds. Serve.

If you prefer to have more sauce, simply double the quantity of the ingredients. This dish is good to serve with plain cooked rice.

粟
米
魚
茸
羹

PEPPERY SHRIMPS
A spicy version of a
popular Cantonese dish
which makes an excellent
starting point for the
beginner in Chinese
cuisine. The cuisine of
Canton (Guangdong)
Province, with its
emphasis on seafood, is
the foundation of Hong
Kong-style cooking

CREAM OF SWEET CORN AND
FISH SOUP
A simple dish with very
full flavour brought out
by the addition of
coriander, which also
serves a decorative
purpose.

葱
花
蒸
蝦

STEAMED PRAWNS WITH SPRING ONIONS AND LIGHT SOY SAUCE

1kg (2lb) prawns (8-10cm/3-4in)
1l (40fl oz/5 cups) boiling water
4 tbsp peanut oil
2 tbsp chopped spring onions
2 garlic cloves

Sauce
2 tbsp light soy sauce
2 tsp Chinese yellow wine
4 tbsp chicken stock

Slit the prawns open along the back and devein them. Clean and pat them dry and arrange them neatly on a plate.

Bring the water to the boil in a wok with a rack in it. Place the plate on the rack and cover the wok. Steam the prawns over a high heat for 5-7 minutes. Remove the plate from the wok and drain all accumulated liquid away from the prawns. Sprinkle chopped spring onions over the prawns and set aside.

Heat the oil in a pan and add the crushed garlic. When the garlic turns brown, drain off the excess oil.

Blend the sauce ingredients and add them to the pan. When the sauce is hot, pour it over the prawns and serve.

THREE DELICACIES STUFFED WITH SHRIMPS

1 aubergine
4 green peppers
4 tomatoes
40g (1½oz) pork fat
300g (11oz) fresh shelled shrimps

Seasonings
1 egg white
1 tsp cornflour
½ tsp salt
¼ tsp peppers

few drops of sesame oil

2 tbsp cornflour
2 tbsp peanut oil

Sauce
1 tbsp tomato juice
2 tsp ketchup
2 tsp soy sauce
5 tbsp chicken stock
1 tsp sugar

Cut the aubergine into slices 1cm (½in) thick and cut a slit in each piece.

Cut the green peppers in half and remove the seeds, and cut the tomatoes in half and remove the pulp.

Dice the pork fat finely. Chop and mash the shrimps into a paste, continuing to stir and beat the paste until it becomes sticky. Add the diced pork fat and continue to stir, and then mix the seasonings with the shrimp paste. Refrigerate for 2 hours.

Coat the inside of the aubergine, green peppers and tomatoes with cornflour and stuff them with the shrimp mixture.

Heat the pan over a high heat. Add 2 tbsp oil and fry the auber-

gine, green peppers and tomatoes, open side down, over a medium heat for 1½ minutes.

Mix and blend the sauce ingredients in a bowl and pour the mixture evenly over the stuffed vegetables. Cover the pan and cook for 2 more minutes, then serve piping hot.

An exotic variant of this dish uses bitter melon, large red chillies and bean curd instead of tomatoes and aubergines.

STEAMED EGG WHITE TOPPED WITH CRAB MEAT AND SHRIMP SAUCE

6 egg whites
225ml (8fl oz/1 cup) chicken stock
1 tbsp cornflour
1 tsp salt

Marinade
1 tbsp egg white
1 tsp cornflour
⅛ tsp pepper

100g (4oz) shrimps
2 tbsp peanut oil

3-4 slices ginger
100g (4oz) crab meat

Sauce
½ cup chicken stock
1 tsp salt
2 tsp Chinese yellow wine
1½ tbsp cornflour

Garnish
1 tbsp chopped coriander

Place the 6 egg whites, chicken stock, cornflour and salt in a bowl. Beat the ingredients with a fork in one direction until they are thoroughly mixed and blended and transfer the mixture to a large, deep-sided dish. Steam the mixture over a medium heat for 5-6 minutes until it has set. Set aside.

Prepare the marinade and mix it with the shrimps. Heat 2 tbsp peanut oil and add the ginger, discarding the ginger when it browns. Add the shrimps and crab meat to the pan. Stir rapidly.

Mix together the sauce ingredients and add to the pan. Keep on stirring. When the contents boil, pour them on top of the steamed egg white. Garnish with chopped coriander and serve.

PAN-FRIED EGG DUMPLING WITH MINCED PORK AND SHRIMPS

6 eggs

Marinade
1 tbsp egg white (from main recipe)
1 tsp salt
1 tsp cornflour
½ tsp sesame oil

100g (4oz) fillet of pork, minced
225g (8oz) shrimps, shelled and
*   deveined*
1 medium onion
225ml (8fl oz/1 cup) peanut oil
1 tbsp chopped coriander

(Recipe continued on page 36)

葱花蒸蝦

STEAMED PRAWNS WITH SPRING
ONIONS AND LIGHT SOY SAUCE
Cantonese chefs are
famous for their steamed
seafood. Here the essence
of the dish lies in the
combination of precise
cooking time and the
last-minute addition of
subtle seasoning elements
to maintain the freshness
of the ingredients.

STEAMED EGG-WHITE TOPPED
WITH CRAB MEAT AND SHRIMP
SAUCE
This is a comparatively
new dish created by
Cantonese chefs in Hong
Kong restaurants to meet
the tastes of a more
health-conscious clientele.
In both taste and
presentation it echoes the
current trend towards
lightness and elegance in
Hong Kong food.

夏令小炒

STIR-FRIED SHRIMP AND
CHICKEN WITH ONION,
CUCUMBER AND FRESH
MUSHROOMS

This colourful stir-fried
dish brings together
ingredients of different
colour, taste and texture.
The Chinese look for
interesting contrasts in
their food, whether in
flavour or texture, but
expect these contrasts to
be harmoniously
combined.

THREE DELICACIES STUFFED
WITH SHRIMPS

In this dish the elements
of contrast are present to
a marked degree in
flavours that are both rich
and delicate. The bitter
melon, particularly,
provides a counterpoint
to the fullness of the chilli
and shrimp.

Break the eggs into a mixing bowl, reserving 1 tbsp egg white for the marinade. Beat the remainder lightly. Make the marinade in a separate bowl and mix the minced pork with half of the mixture.

Clean the shrimps. Pat them dry and mix with the other half of the marinade. Keep refrigerated for 30 minutes.

Chop the onion and set it aside.

Heat the oil in a pan. Add the shrimps, stirring to separate, and remove them when their colour has changed.Drain and set aside.

Sauté the minced pork for 2 minutes. Remove and set aside. Sauté the chopped onion for 1 minute. Remove and set aside.

Mix the pork, shrimps, onion and coriander with the beaten egg. Heat 1 tbsp oil in the pan and put 2 tbsp of the egg mixture in the pan to form one dumpling. Fry it gently over a medium heat, turning it over gently until both sides are nicely golden brown. Make two or three at a time and continue until all the ingredients are used. This simple but effective recipe will make eight or ten dumplings in all.

SHRIMP, HAM AND MELON ROLLS

200g (7oz) shrimps, freshly shelled (if not available, use frozen shrimps)

Seasonings

½ tsp salt

2 tsp cornflour

½ tsp chopped garlic

25g (1oz) belly of pork

50g (2oz) ham

600g (1½lb) winter melon

Sauce

2 tbsp peanut oil

2 pieces of sliced ginger

1 tsp finely chopped garlic

8 tbsp stock

2 tsp soy sauce

2 tsp oyster sauce

few drops of sesame oil

3 tsp rice wine

½ tsp cornflour (blended in water)

Chop and mince the shrimps. Mix the seasonings with the shrimps and beat the mixture until it is sticky.

Dice the belly of pork into tiny cubes and chop and mince the ham. Mix both with the shrimp mixture.

Cut the winter melon into pieces 3 × 5 × 10cm (1½ × 2 × 4in) and blanch the melon in boiling water. Remove and drain.

Spread a little of the shrimp mixture on each melon slice. Roll the melon around the mixture and place the rolls on a plate standing on a metal rack in a large saucepan. Steam the rolls vigorously for 10 minutes.

Make the sauce by heating 2 tbsp peanut oil in a pan. Add the ginger slices but remove them as soon as they become yellow. Then add the garlic and the other sauce ingredients. Stir when the sauce boils, stir again and pour over the melon rolls to serve.

桂
林
蝦
丸

DEEP-FRIED SHRIMP BALLS SERVED WITH SWEET-AND-SOUR SAUCE

500g (1¼lb) shrimps, shelled and deveined	1 egg white
50g (2oz) pork back fat	2 tbsp cornflour
50g (2oz) water chestnut	200g (7oz) breadcrumbs
	450ml (16floz/2 cups) peanut oil

Clean the shrimps. Pat them dry and beat them with the flat side of a cleaver.

Dice the cooked pork fat into tiny pieces and cut the water chestnuts into similar tiny pieces.

Put the beaten shrimps in a mixing bowl and add the egg white and cornflour. Stir with a fork in one direction until the mixture is sticky and firm.

Add the pork fat and keep on stirring until the mixture is consistent and sticky. Stir in the diced pieces of water chestnut and keep on stirring until the mixture becomes firm.

Lightly oil your fingers and palms and roll ¾ tbsp of the shrimp mixture into a small ball. Coat each ball with breadcrumbs.

Heat the oil in a pan. Test that the temperature is correct by putting a thin slice of ginger into the pan; when it curls up immediately the temperature is right. Add the shrimp balls and fry over a high heat for 1 minute. Reduce the temperature to medium and fry for another 2 minutes. Turn off the heat and let the shrimp balls sit for 5 minutes in the oil. Remove and drain.

Reheat the oil and after 15 seconds return the shrimp balls and fry for 2 minutes. Serve with Sweet-and-sour Sauce (see below).

SWEET-AND-SOUR SAUCE BASE

1l (40floz/5 cups) rice vinegar	338ml (12floz/1½ cups) tomato ketchup
2 tsp salt	
450g (1lb) brown sugar	2 tsp dark soy sauce

This recipe makes a useful sweet-and-sour sauce base that will keep for long periods.

Bring the vinegar to the boil. Add the salt and then add the sugar. Once the sugar has dissolved, add the tomato ketchup. When the mixture returns to the boil, add the soy sauce.

This sauce base can be kept in the refrigerator in a covered container until needed. For use and to serve, add water and cornflour and bring to the boil, stirring all the time until the sauce thickens and becomes translucent. It may be served with such dishes as sweet-and-sour-pork, spare ribs and deep-fried fish.

煎蛋角

PAN-FRIED EGG DUMPLING

DEEP-FRIED SHRIMP BALLS
Deep-fried dishes such as this are familiar favourites in the west. A serving of sweet-and-sour sauce adds a complementary contrast of flavour.

PAN-FRIED EGG DUMPLING WITH MINCED PORK AND SHRIMPS
This is really a type of Chinese omelette, but with an extra succulence and delicacy. Patience is the key to success in this dish — use low heat to avoid burning the dumplings.

SHRIMP, HAM AND MELON ROLLS
This dish has been aptly described as a new frontier in taste. Elegant and exotic to look at, it provides a deliciously surprising flavour that can be enjoyed at little risk to the waistline!

桂林蝦丸

SHARK'S FIN CONSOMME

600g (1½lb) shark's fin	*3 slices ginger*
50g (2oz) ham	*225ml (8floz/1 cup) good stock*
600g (1½lb) lean pork	*1½ tbsp ham, finely shredded*
1.25l (48floz/6 cups) chicken stock	*1½ tbsp chopped coriander*

Soak the dried shark's fin in 2l (4 pints) boiling water overnight. The next day bring 4l (1 gallon) water to the boil and simmer the shark's fin for 6 hours. Remove it from the water and rinse under the tap for 30-60 minutes.

Blanch 50g (2oz) ham and the lean pork in 1l (40floz/5 cups) boiling water for 5 minutes, then place the meat, the chicken stock and ginger in a covered china container and steam for 3 hours.

Place the prepared shark's fin on a platter, add 225ml (8floz/1 cup) good stock and steam for 20 minutes.

Divide the shark's fin into small individual portions, add the boiling stock and sprinkle with the finely shredded ham and chopped coriander. Serve.

SHARK'S FIN SOUP WITH CHICKEN WING STUFFED WITH HAM AND MUSHROOMS

600g (1½lb) dried shark's fin, skin and bone removed	*100g (4oz) ham*
	10 chicken wings
1l (2 pints/5 cups) chicken stock	*2 large black mushrooms*
600g (1½lb) spare rib of pork	

Prepare the shark's fin, following the method given in the recipe for Shark's Fin Consommé. Set it aside.

Bring the chicken stock and an equal amount of water to the boil. Add the spare rib of pork and 70g (2½oz) ham cut into thin slices. Simmer for 2 hours and set aside.

Steam the chicken wings for 20 minutes, remove the bones and set aside.

Soak the mushrooms in hot water for 30 minutes. Remove and discard the stems and cut the caps into 4mm (¼in) strips. Set them aside.

Cut the remaining ham into slices 2mm (⅛in) thick and cut each slice into pieces 2 × 40mm (⅛ × 1¾in). Set them aside.

Stuff the chicken wings with strips of mushroom and ham, place the shark's fin in a soup tureen and arrange the stuffed chicken wings on top.

Add the stock and steam for 1 hour. Serve.

蟹
黃
魚
翅

SHARK'S FIN SOUP WITH CRAB ROE SAUCE

600g (1½lb) dried shark's fin, skin
    and bone removed
225ml (8fl oz/1 cup) peanut oil
6 slices ginger
1 stalk spring onion
roe from 2 female crabs
1 tsp sesame oil

1 tbsp Chinese yellow wine
900ml (32fl oz/4 cups) chicken
    stock
1 tsp salt
2 tbsp cornflour, softened in 2 tbsp
    water

Prepare the shark's fin, following the method given in the recipe for Shark's Fin Consommé. Set it aside.

Heat two-thirds of the oil in a pan and add the ginger and spring onion. Remove them when they have browned and turn off the heat.

Mix 3 tbsp oil with the crab roes, add the sesame oil and Chinese yellow wine, stir well and set aside.

Reheat the oil, add the shark's fin and chicken stock and simmer for 30 minutes. Add the salt and simmer for a further 5 minutes. Bring the contents of the pan to the boil again and stir in 2 tbsp cornflour mixed with an equal amount of water. Reduce the heat, stir in the crab roes and serve.

SHARK'S FIN WITH CRAB MEAT IN BROWN SAUCE

600g (1½lb) dried shark's fin, skin
    and bone removed
8 tbsp peanut oil
4 slices ginger
1 spring onion
900ml (32fl oz/4 cups) chicken
    stock
225g (8oz) crab meat
1½ tbsp Chinese yellow wine

1 tbsp oyster sauce
1 tsp sugar
1 tbsp light soy sauce
½ tsp pepper
1 tsp sesame oil
2 tbsp cornflour softened in 2 tbsp
    water
1 tsp dark soy sauce

Prepare the shark's fin, following the method given in the recipe for Shark's Fin Consomme. Set it aside.

Heat the peanut oil in a pan. Add the ginger and spring onion, but remove and discard them when they turn brown.

Add the shark's fin and the chicken stock to the pan and bring the mixture to the boil over medium heat. Add the crab meat and reduce the temperature to low.

When the mixture boils again add 1 tsp Chinese yellow wine and the oyster sauce, sugar, light soy sauce, pepper and sesame oil. Stir in the softened cornflour, add the dark soy sauce and 1 tbsp Chinese yellow wine and serve.

清
湯
魚
翅

SHARK'S FIN SOUP WITH
CHICKEN WING STUFFED WITH
HAM AND MUSHROOMS
A traditional delicacy in
modern style, this soup is
a feast of flavour and
refinement. Shark's fin
may be bought in
semi-finished form in
Chinese food shops but
the process of
preparation is still a long
one. The effort, however,
is richly repaid by the
compliments of one's
guests.

SHARK'S FIN CONSOMME
This classic dish is
appreciated by
connoisseurs of Chinese
cuisine for its clarity,
flavour and the distinctive
glutinous texture of the
shark's fin.

蟹
黃
魚
翅

SHARK'S FIN WITH CRAB MEAT IN BROWN SAUCE
In this treatment of a traditional delicacy, the sweetness of the crab meat, with its colour, provides a visual and full-flavoured contrast with the shark's fin.

SHARK'S FIN SOUP WITH CRAB ROE SAUCE
In Chinese culture, this delicious shark's fin dish symbolizes prosperity. It is always the star of a Chinese New Year banquet menu, where it appears as 'Prosperous Shark's Fin'.

董
葱
焗
蟹

CRAB CASSEROLE

2 crabs (approximately 500g (1¼lb) each	**Seasonings**
	8 tbsp good stock
1 tbsp cornflour	1 tbsp oyster sauce
½l (20fl oz/3 cups) peanut oil (to fry crabs)	1 tsp oil
	few drops sesame oil
2 tsp chopped garlic	1 tsp sugar
3-4 slices root ginger	1 tsp rice wine
2 stalks spring onions	

Clean the crabs and crush the pincers. Chop each crab into six pieces. Dry and dust with cornflour.

Heat the peanut oil and fry the crabs for 1 minute. Remove the crab from the pan and drain the oil.

Heat a large pan or wok. Add the garlic, ginger and spring onions and sauté for 15 seconds to release their aromatic flavours. Mix and turn them quickly with the crab before transferring the mixture to a clay container or casserole.

Add the seasonings. Cover the pot and cook for 2 minutes over a high heat, turning the contents from time to time.

Serve in the clay pot or casserole.

STIR-FRIED CRAB IN CURRY SAUCE

1kg (2lb) crab	5cm (2in) pieces
2 tbsp cornflour	1 tbsp curry paste
450ml (16fl oz/2 cups) peanut oil	225ml (8fl oz/1 cup) chicken stock
6 slices ginger	2 tsp sugar
2 tsp chopped garlic	1 tsp salt
100g (4oz) spring onions, cut into	1 tsp Chinese yellow wine

Place the crab on a chopping-board, belly-side up, and cut through the middle with a cleaver, but avoid cutting into the top shell. Chop off the claws, lightly crush the shell and set them aside. Lift off the top shell and clean the crab, discarding the 'dead men's fingers'. Chop the body into four or six pieces, depending on the size, and lightly coat the crab meat with cornflour.

Heat the oil in a pan and fry the crab for 2 minutes over a very high heat. Remove, drain and set aside.

Heat 2 tbsp oil in the pan. Add the ginger, garlic, spring onion and curry paste, stir and cook for 1½ minutes.

Return the crab to the pan, stirring, and add the chicken stock, sugar and salt. Cover the pan and cook over medium heat for 10 minutes, turning the contents once or twice to ensure that they are evenly cooked. Sprinkle with yellow wine and serve.

鼓
椒
炒
蟹

CRAB WITH FERMENTED BEANS AND PEPPERS

2 crabs (approximately 450g (1lb) each)
2 red chilli peppers
1 green bell pepper
4 pieces ginger
3 stalks spring onions
2 garlic cloves
450ml (16floz/2 cups) peanut oil (for frying crab)
3 tsp salted, fermented soya beans

Seasoning
1 tsp sugar
1 tsp salt
2 tsp oyster sauce
1/2 tsp monosodium glutamate (optional)
2 tsp rice wine

8 tbsp stock or chicken soup

Clean the crabs and chop the flesh of each into six pieces.

Mince the chilli and the green pepper. Slice the ginger and cut the spring onions into 2cm (3/4in) pieces. Crush and chop garlic.

Heat the oil in a pan and add the crab, ginger and spring onions. Fry for 2 minutes and remove from the pan to drain.

Reheat the pan to smoking point and add 1 tbsp oil. Fry the garlic and beans for 10 seconds, then return the crab to the pan.

Mix the seasoning ingredients with the stock or chicken soup and add the mixture to the pan. Turn and stir the contents for 30 seconds and serve.

ASPARAGUS TOPPED WITH CRAB MEAT SAUCE

100g (4oz) crab meat
500g (1¼lb) fresh asparagus
4 tbsp peanut oil
8 tbsp chicken stock
4 slices ginger
1 garlic clove

Sauce
1 egg white
8 tbsp chicken stock
1 tsp sesame oil
2 tsp Chinese yellow wine
1/2 tsp sugar
1/4 tsp pepper
1 1/2 tsp cornflour

Steam a medium sized crab for 20 minutes. Scoop out the crab meat from the shells and set aside.

Clean the asparagus and cut the stalks into 3cm (1½in) sections, discarding the tough part close to the roots.

Heat 1 tbsp oil and add the chicken stock to the pan. Cook the asparagus until the stock is almost dried up. Transfer to a plate and set aside to keep warm.

Heat 3 tbsp oil in the pan, add the ginger and garlic and when browned, remove and discard them.

Add the crab meat to the pan and sauté for 30 seconds. Mix the sauce ingredients, stir into the pan and bring to the boil. Pour the mixture over the asparagus and serve.

香汁炒蟹

STIR-FRIED CRAB IN CURRY SAUCE

There is an obvious south-east Asian influence in this Cantonese dish. Although, in general, Cantonese cuisine is subtle in character, there are hot and spicy dishes comparable to the Sichuan school.

CRAB CASSEROLE

A superb dish for the colder months of the year. The delicate flavour is typical of the Cantonese school.

豉椒炒蟹

CRAB WITH FERMETED BEANS AND PEPPERS

Fermented beans, more commonly known as black beans, are widely used in Cantonese cooking, usually with red chilli and garlic. Together they make a unique spicy sauce that is unmistakably Cantonese.

蠔汁鮑片

ABALONE STEAK IN OYSTER SAUCE

2 tins abalone	*1 tbsp Chinese yellow wine*
3-4 tbsp peanut oil	*2 tbsp oyster sauce*
3-4 slices ginger	*1 tsp sugar*
1-2 garlic cloves	*2 tbsp cornflour*

Boil the abalone in the tins for 5 hours over a low heat in 3-4 l (6-7 pints) of water before opening the tins. Cut the abalone in slices 1 cm ($\frac{1}{2}$ in) thick. Save 8 tbsp of liquid in the tins as a base for the sauce.

Heat 3-4 tbsp oil in a pan and add the ginger and garlic, frying them until browned. Remove and discard.

Add the Chinese yellow wine and liquid from the abalone to the pan and stir in the oyster sauce, sugar and cornflour mixed with 2 tbsp water.

Finally, add the abalone slices, stir well to mix with the sauce and serve.

Abalone is always one of the star dishes on a banquet menu. Tinned abalone is recommended for this recipe as some of the dried varieties are expensive and complicated to prepare. If you wish you may take the abalone from the tin without first boiling it, but you will have to cut it into thinner slices, not exceeding 3 mm ($\frac{1}{8}$ in), or the texture will be too tough and rubbery for you to enjoy.

SLICED ABALONE IN OYSTER SAUCE WITH LETTUCE

500g (1$\frac{1}{4}$lb) tinned abalone	*2 tbsp oyster sauce*
140ml (5fl oz/generous $\frac{1}{2}$ cup)	*1 tsp dark soy sauce*
* peanut oil*	*1 tsp sesame oil*
1 tbsp salt	*1 tsp sugar*
500g (1$\frac{1}{4}$lb) lettuce	*4 tbsp chicken stock*
2-3 slices ginger	*4 tbsp abalone stock*
1-2 garlic cloves	*1 tsp Chinese yellow wine*
1 tbsp Chinese yellow wine	*1 tbsp cornflour*

Stand the unopened tin of abalone in plenty of water and boil for 3 hours. Remove the abalone from the tin, saving 4 tbsp juice to make the sauce. Trim the abalone into thin slices (2-10mm/ $\frac{1}{8}$-$\frac{1}{2}$in) and set aside.

Heat 4 tbsp oil and the salt with 900ml (32fl oz/4 cups) water in a pan. Bring to the boil and blanch the lettuce leaves for 1 minute. Remove, drain thoroughly and place on a serving dish.

Heat 6 tbsp oil in the pan and add the ginger and garlic.

Remove and discard the garlic when it has turned brown. Add the abalone slices and 1 tbsp Chinese yellow wine and sauté them lightly.

Add the remaining ingredients, stir and cook for 30 seconds over medium heat. Transfer to the serving dish with the lettuce.

You can make this dish more saucy by using all the abalone stock from the tin and doubling the portions of the other sauce ingredients.

ABALONE, CHICKEN AND DUCK WRAPPED IN LETTUCE LEAVES

40g (1½oz) abalone
40g (1½oz) breast of chicken
40g (1½oz) roast duck
40g (1½oz) fresh chicken liver
25g (1oz) water chestnuts
2 large button mushrooms
3 stalks spring onion
450ml (16floz/2 cups) peanut oil
40g (1½oz) olive kernels
10g (½oz) rice-flour noodles
1 tsp chopped garlic
1 tsp chopped ginger

Seasonings
1 tsp oyster sauce

1 tsp monosodium glutamate (optional)
½ tsp salt
½ tsp sugar
¼ tsp pepper
4 tbsp stock

25g (1oz) cooked ham, chopped
2 stalks Chinese parsley or coriander leaves
10 lettuce leaves
1 dish containing 3 tbsp hoisin sauce
1 dish containing 1 tbsp shredded ginger and 2 tbsp vinegar

Dice the abalone, chicken, duck, chicken liver, water chestnuts and mushrooms into 1cm (½in) cubes. Cut the spring onion into pieces 2cm (¾in) long.

Heat a pan until it is very hot and pour the peanut oil into it. Fry the chicken, chicken liver and olive kernels for 15 seconds. Remove them from the pan, leaving behind the oil. Reheat the oil and add the rice noodles to the same pan. They should froth up into crispy noodles.

Remove them from the pan and drain on absorbent paper. Spread out the noodles on a serving dish.

Heat the pan again until it is very hot. Add 2 tbsp peanut oil. When hot, add the onions, garlic and ginger, and then the water chestnuts and mushrooms. Stir-fry for 1 minute. Add the abalone, chicken meat, duck meat, chicken liver, olive kernels and the seasonings. Stir-fry for another minute. Transfer from the pan to the plate, arranging them on top of the rice noodles. Garnish with the chopped ham and parsley or coriander.

The dish is eaten by wrapping spoonfuls of the dish in the lettuce leaves, which are spread with hoisin sauce and sprinkled with vinegar and ginger.

蟹扒露笋

ASPARAGUS TOPPED WITH CRAB
MEAT SAUCE
Chinese chefs are famous
for preparing vegetables
in such a way as to
maintain freshness and
flavour. Here, the
combination of asparagus
and crab meat offers a
particularly successful
harmony of flavours.

SLICED ABALONE IN OYSTER
SAUCE WITH LETTUCE
Properly prepared,
abalone is a great delicacy
and is deservedly one of
the highlights of the
Chinese banquet menu.
The rich oyster sauce in
this dish enhances both
the flavour and texture of
the abalone.

蟹
扒
露
笋

ABALONE, CHICKEN AND DUCK
WRAPPED IN LETTUCE
A good example of the
way in which Chinese
cooking makes optimum
use of ingredients. The
trimmings of abalone
steak inject new life into
this otherwise rather
ordinary dish. The
combination is set off by
the freshness and
crispiness of the lettuce.

ABALONE STEAK IN OYSTER
SAUCE
Abalone is unashamedly a
luxury item and a piece of
best-quality abalone steak
in a Hong Kong
restaurant would cost as
much as a meal for two in
London!

51

酥炸生蠔

FRIED OYSTER

12 large oysters
2 tbsp cornflour (for cleaning
    oysters)
2 tbsp salt (for cleaning oysters)
1 tsp monosodium glutamate
    (optional)
1 tsp salt

Sauce
50g (2oz) wheat flour
2 tbsp cornflour

20g (¾oz) powdered yeast
1 tsp oil
170ml (6floz/¾ cup) water

450ml (16floz/2 cups) peanut oil
    (for frying oysters)

Dips
1 small plate of ketchup
1 small plate of spiced salt

Rub the oysters thoroughly with cornflour and salt and then wash them in water. Drop the oysters into a pan of boiling water until they are half cooked (this takes about 20 seconds). Dry the oysters carefully with a towel then mix them well with the monosodium glutamate (if used) and 1 tsp salt.

Mix the sauce ingredients, blending them together thoroughly.

Heat the peanut oil in a pan. Dip the oysters into the sauce and fry them until brown over low heat.

Serve with ketchup, or prepare a dish of spiced salt by putting 1-2 tbsp salt and 1 tsp peppercorns in a pan over low heat until they start to brown; remove the peppercorns and keep the salt.

STIR-FRIED SCALLOPS WITH SNOW PEAS, CELERY, WATER CHESTNUTS AND BLACK FUNGUS

450g (1lb) scallops (fresh or
    frozen)

Marinade
1 tsp salt
½ tsp pepper
1 tsp sesame oil
1¼ tbsp ginger juice
1 tbsp cornflour

25g (1oz) dried black fungus
    (cloud ear)
225g (8oz) snow pea
225g (8oz) celery
100g (4oz) water chestnut

450ml (16floz/2 cups) peanut oil
1 tsp salt
2 tbsp stock
2 tsp minced ginger
2 tsp minced garlic

Sauce
1 tbsp oyster sauce
1 tsp dark soy sauce
1 tbsp light soy sauce
2 tbsp stock
1 tsp sugar
½ tsp sesame oil
1 tbsp cornflour
2 tsp Chinese yellow wine

Cut the scallops horizontally in half. Mix the marinade ingredients and add the scallops. Set aside.

Soak the black fungus in hot water for about 10 minutes.

Top and tail the snow peas, cutting them slantwise into 5 × 2cm (2 × ³/₄in) pieces. Cut the celery into pieces the same size. Slice the water chestnut into 5mm (¹/₄in) pieces.

Heat the oil in a pan until very hot: test by putting in a thin slice of ginger; if it curls up and browns immediately the temperature is right. Add the scallops, stirring to separate and prevent them from sticking. Turn off the heat and allow to stand for 30 seconds. Drain thoroughly and set aside.

Heat 2 tbsp oil in the pan. Add the snow peas, celery, water chestnut and black fungus, sauté and stir for 1 minute. Add 1 tsp salt and 2 tbsp stock and cook for another minute. Remove from the pan and set aside. Heat 1 tbsp oil in the pan. Add the ginger and garlic and, when the aroma rises, add the scallops and other ingredients. Stir rapidly over a high heat for 15 seconds.

Mix the sauce ingredients and add to the pan. Stir rapidly for another 15 seconds and serve.

STEAMED GROUPER WITH HAM AND MUSHROOMS

600-800g (1¹/₂-1³/₄lb) grouper or sea bass	150g (5oz) ham
2 tsp salt	4 slices root-ginger
¹/₄ tsp pepper	4 stalks spring onion
6 tbsp peanut oil	2 tbsp light soy sauce
12 medium Chinese dried mushrooms	2 tbsp Chinese rice wine or dry sherry

Clean the fish, remove the bones and cut the flesh into about 12 evenly sized pieces. Mix the salt and pepper with 2 tsp oil and rub the mixture over the fish pieces.

Soak the dried mushrooms in hot water for 30 minutes. Remove and discard the stems and cut the caps slantwise into three thin slices. Cut the ham into thin slices of similar size.

Shred the ginger and spring onion into matchstick-size pieces and arrange half of the pieces as a bed on an oval, heatproof plate. Place the fish pieces, alternating with slices of ham and mushroom, over the ginger and spring onion and put the plate in a steamer. Steam vigorously for 10 minutes and pour away any excess liquid that has accumulated during the steaming.

Sprinkle the soy sauce and rice wine over the fish, ham and mushroom and lay the remaining spring onion shreds on top.

Heat 5 tbsp oil in a small pan and add the remaining shredded ginger. Stir the ginger in the boiling oil for 30 seconds, remove and discard the ginger and pour the hot oil over the fish, ham and mushroom. Serve.

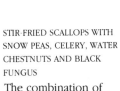

FRIED OYSTER

FRIED OYSTER

This is not unlike the western oyster fritter. Worcestershire sauce is an essential ingredient which gives the seafood the required fiery bite.

STIR-FRIED SCALLOPS WITH SNOW PEAS, CELERY, WATER CHESTNUTS AND BLACK FUNGUS

The combination of vegetables used here appeals to both eye and palate, providing a skilful contrast of colours, textures and tastes to offset seafood, meat or poultry.

雲腿麒麟斑

STEAMED GROUPER WITH HAM AND MUSHROOMS
The fish is cooked here in the classical Cantonese manner. First it is cooked with a heavy dressing of freshly shredded ginger and spring onion. This layer is then removed and a fresh layer of the same vegetables is laid over it. At this point a quantity of superheated fat or oil is poured over the length of the fish to impact the flavour of the ginger and spring onion into the fish. Here the carved slices of fish are interleaved with slices of dried mushroom and ham, which further enhance the flavour of this popular and colourful party dish.

FISH SOUP WITH BEAN CURD, VEGETABLES AND FISH ROLLS

600g (1½lb) sole (use a fillet of 225g (8oz) for fish rolls (below), the rest for making the soup)
225g (8oz) spinach
2 cakes bean curd
1 tbsp peanut oil
4 pieces sliced ginger

750ml (1¼ pint/3½ cups) chicken stock

Seasoning
⅛ tsp white pepper
½ tsp salt
1 tsp monosodium glutamate (optional)

Remove the fillet from the fish to make the rolls and chop the remainder into smaller pieces to make the soup.

Clean the spinach thoroughly and cut it into pieces 5cm (2in) long. Divide each cake of bean curd into four pieces.

Heat the oil in the pan. Add the ginger and the fish bones and trimmings to sauté for 1 minute. Add the chicken stock and the same quantity of water to the pan, adding the bean curd when the stock boils.

Boil for 7 minutes, add the vegetables and boil for another 3 minutes. Add the seasoning and serve with fish rolls (see below).

FISH ROLLS

225g (8oz) filleted sole
4 medium dried black mushrooms
¼ tsp salt
1 tsp oil

Seasonings
½ tsp salt
1½ tsp cornflour
½ egg white

25g (1oz) ham
40g (1½oz) bamboo shoots

450ml(16floz/2 cups) peanut oil (to fry fish rolls)
½ tsp chopped garlic
½ tsp chopped ginger

Sauce
2 tbsp stock
1 tbsp oyster sauce
2 tsp soy sauce
1 tsp rice wine
1 tsp cornflour

Cut the fish into pieces approximately 4 × 6cm (1¾ × 2½in).

Soak the mushrooms in a small bowl of hot water for 30 minutes. Add ¼ tsp salt and 1 tsp of oil to the mushrooms and steam them for 10 minutes. Shred the mushrooms, discarding the stems.

Mix the seasoning ingredients and coat the fish thoroughly with the mixture.

Slice the ham and the bamboo shoots to matchstick-size shreds about 2cm (¾in) long.

Place a combination of the ham, bamboo shoots and mushrooms in the centre of each fish fillet. Roll the fish up around the mixture and dust with flour.

魚
卷
連
湯

Heat the peanut oil until very hot and fry a few fish rolls for 10-20 seconds until they become golden. Remove and set aside. Repeat until all the fish rolls are fried.

Reheat the pan until it is very hot and pour in 1 tbsp peanut oil. Add the garlic and ginger to sauté. Return the fish rolls to the pan. Mix the sauce ingredients and add to the pan, turning the fish rolls over in the boiling sauce over a high heat for 10 seconds. Serve as an accompaniment to soup.

STEAMED SEA BASS WITH BLACK MUSHROOMS AND CHINESE HAM

600g (1½lb) fillet of sea bass or any white fish

Marinade
1 egg white
1 tsp cornflour
½ tsp sesame oil
⅛ tsp pepper
1 tsp salt

6 medium black mushrooms
50g (2oz) Chinese ham

6 stalks spring onions
6 slices ginger, shredded
8 tbsp peanut oil
1 garlic clove

Sauce
1 tbsp oyster sauce
1 tbsp light soy sauce
½ tsp sugar
1 tsp sesame oil
1 tsp Chinese yellow wine
225ml (8floz/1 cup) chicken stock

Clean the fish and cut it into slices 50 × 30 × 5mm (2 × 1½ × ¼in). Mix the marinade, add the fish pieces and set aside.

Soak the black mushrooms in hot water for 30 minutes. Remove and discard the stems and cut each mushroom into three or four slices. Set these aside.

Cut the ham into thin slices, about the same size as the fish pieces, and set aside.

Take four of the spring onions, cutting them into 3cm (1½in) pieces. Use only the white part and the part immediately next to it, discarding the roots and discoloured stalks.

Place the remaining two spring onions on a large plate. Arrange the fish, ham and mushrooms in layers — one piece of fish, one piece of ham, one piece of black mushroom — on top of the spring onions until all the fish, ham and mushroom is used. Sprinkle the chopped spring onion and shredded ginger on top of them.

Bring 900ml (32floz/4 cups) water to the boil in a wok. Put a wire rack in the wok and put the plate on top. Steam vigorously over a high heat for 5-7 minutes only.

Remove the plate of fish from the wok, drain, and set aside.

Heat the oil in a pan. Add the garlic but remove it when it has browned and discard it. Pour the oil over the fish, draining away any excess from the plate. Add all the sauce ingredients to a pan, stir and bring to the boil. Pour over the fish and serve.

脆皮魚卷

FISH SOUP WITH BEAN CURD,
VEGETABLES AND FISH ROLLS
Chinese cooks abhor
waste. This recipe, which
uses one fish for two
dishes, will meet with the
approval of the
budget-conscious.

SMOKED WHITE FISH FRENCH
STYLE
Not strictly speaking
French, this dish is a
Hong Kong interpretation
of a French classic recipe.

雲腿麒麟斑

STEAMED SEA BASS WITH BLACK MUSHROOMS AND CHINESE HAM
Chinese black mushrooms, ginger and soy sauce are sufficient to give an authentic Chinese flavour to an everyday meal. If sea bass is not available, other fish may be substituted.

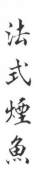

SMOKED WHITE FISH FRENCH STYLE

800g (1¾lb) white fish, such as turbot

Seasonings
4 soupspoons western sauce
¼ tsp white pepper
1 tsp onion powder
1 tsp sugar
1 tsp sherry

1 tbsp butter

Garnish
half a lettuce
2 tomatoes
4 pieces ham (about 100g (4oz) each)
2-3 tbsp mayonnaise

Cut the fish into four big pieces. Mix the seasonings together and marinate the fish in the mixture for 7-8 hours or overnight.

Drain the fish and bake it in a moderate oven (180°C/350°F/Gas Mark 4) for 15 minutes. Butter the fish on both sides and bake for a further 10 minutes. Shred the lettuce and slice the tomatoes. Halve each piece of ham. Put the fish on a hot plate and garnish with lettuce, tomatoes, ham and mayonnaise.

To make western sauce, finely shred 100g (4oz) each of celery, carrot and onion and 2 bay leaves. Add the shredded vegetables to 225ml (8fl oz/1cup) chicken stock and cook over medium heat until the liquid has reduced by about 50 per cent.

STEAMED CHICKEN AND FROGS' LEGS WRAPPED IN LOTUS LEAVES

450g (1lb) chicken legs
225g (8oz) frogs' legs

Marinade
1 egg white
1 tsp salt
1 tbsp light soy sauce
1 tsp dark soy sauce
1 tsp sugar
2 tsp Chinese yellow wine

1 tbsp cornflour
½ tsp sesame oil

100g (4oz) fresh straw mushrooms
2 spring onions
1-2 lotus leaves (depending on their size)
25g (1oz) ham, sliced
6 slices ginger

Chop the chicken legs into bite-size pieces and cut the frogs' legs in half, discarding the lower leg. Marinate the chicken and frogs' legs and set aside. Cut the straw mushrooms in half and cut the spring onions into 3cm (1½in) sections.

Blanch the dry lotus leaves in 1l (2 pints) boiling water until they are soft, remove, rinse under the tap and pat dry. Put all the ingredients in an even layer on the lotus leaves, wrapping them up firmly and neatly. Place the parcel on a heatproof plate and steam over medium heat for 35 minutes. Unwrap the parcel and trim the lotus leaves to fit the plate. Serve.

蝦
醬
全
雞

GOLDEN CHICKEN WITH SHRIMP PASTE

1½kg (3-3½lb) fresh chicken
2-3 tbsp shrimp paste (fresh
  shrimps finely minced)

Marinade
3 tbsp cornflour

1 tbsp Mei Kwei Lu or dry sherry
2 tsp ginger juice
1 tsp sugar
few drops sesame oil

½l (20floz/3 cups) peanut oil

Chop the chicken into large, bite-size pieces and pat them dry.

Mix the shrimp paste with the marinade ingredients, and marinate the chicken with the mixture for 20 minutes.

Heat the peanut oil in a pan until it is very hot. Put in the chicken pieces and fry them for 2 minutes over a low heat. Remove the chicken and set the pieces aside while you reheat the oil to boiling point. Fry them again for 1½ minutes and serve.

ROAST GOOSE CASSEROLE WITH BAMBOO SHOOTS

300g (10-12oz) roast goose
200g (7oz) bamboo shoots
6 medium black mushrooms
⅓ whole piece of aged dried orange
  peel
1 tbsp peanut oil
6 slices ginger
2-3 garlic cloves, crushed

Sauce
1 tbsp oyster sauce

1 tbsp light soy sauce
1 tsp dark soy sauce
½ tsp sesame oil
2 tsp Chinese yellow wine
225ml (8floz/1 cup) chicken stock

1 tbsp cornflour
spring onion cut into 3cm (1½in)
  lengths
1 tbsp coriander, chopped

Cut the roast goose into bite-size pieces and the bamboo shoots into wedge shapes.

Soak the black mushrooms and dried orange peel in hot water for 30 minutes. Remove and discard the mushroom stems and finely shred the orange peel. Set aside.

Blanch the bamboo shoots in ½l (20floz/3 cups) boiling water for 5 minutes. Remove, rinse under the tap, drain and set aside.

Heat the peanut oil in a clay pot and add the ginger and garlic. When the aroma arises, add the roast goose, bamboo shoots, black mushrooms and orange peel, stir and cook for 1 minute.

Add the sauce ingredients to the pan and enough water to cover the ingredients. Bring to the boil, reduce the heat and simmer for 45 minutes. Thicken the sauce with 1 tbsp cornflour mixed with an equal amount of water. Add the spring onion and coriander and serve.

蝦醬全雞

STEAMED CHICKEN AND
FROGS' LEGS WRAPPED IN
LOTUS LEAVES
A great summer dish
distingished by the
refreshing fragrance of
lotus leaves. The colours
— jade green, ivory and
ruby red — suggest a
Chinese painting.

GOLDEN CHICKEN WITH
SHRIMP PASTE
As in all fried chicken
dishes, the chicken
should be juicy inside
and crispy outside.
Careful heat control is the
key.

62

炒燒鵝鬆

ROAST GOOSE CASSEROLE
WITH BAMBOO SHOOTS
A good way to use the
stringier parts of the bird
which might be tough if
they weren't cut into
small pieces.

CHICKEN, ABALONE, BLACK MUSHROOMS AND BAMBOO SHOOTS IN A CLAY POT

250g (9oz) tinned abalone

Sauce
2 tbsp oyster sauce
1 tbsp light soy sauce
1 tsp dark soy sauce
1 tsp sugar
4 tbsp chicken stock
1 tbsp cornflour

*2 stalks spring onion, cut into 5cm
    (2in) lengths*
500g (1¼lb) chicken drumsticks

Marinade
1 tbsp light soy sauce
½ tsp sugar
1 tsp sesame oil
1 tbsp cornflour

8-10 medium black mushrooms
225g (8oz) bamboo shoots
450ml (16floz/2 cups) peanut oil
1 tsp chopped ginger
1 tsp chopped garlic
225ml (8floz/1 cup) chicken stock
2 tsp Chinese yellow wine

Cut the abalone into slices approximately 5cm (2in) thick. Mix the sauce ingredients in a bowl and add the sliced abalone and spring onions.

Chop the drumsticks into bite-size pieces; marinade them.

Soak the black mushrooms in hot water for 30 minutes. Remove and discard the stems. Cut the bamboo shoots into wedges about 5cm (2in) long.

Heat the oil in a pan. When it is hot, add the chicken and fry for 2 minutes. Remove and set aside.

Heat 2 tbsp oil in a clay pot and add the chopped ginger and garlic. When the aroma rises, add the chicken, black mushrooms and bamboo shoots, stirring all the time. Cook for 1 minute.

Add the chicken stock, bring to the boil, cover and simmer over medium heat for 10 minutes.

Add the sauce ingredients, spring onions and abalone slices. Stir-fry for 30 seconds and sprinkle with 2 tsp Chinese yellow wine before serving.

QUICKLY BRAISED CHICKEN WITH CHILLIES, GREEN PEPPERS AND BLACK BEANS

*1 chicken (approximately
    1¼kg/2½lb)*
3 green bell peppers
2 fresh red chillies
1 small piece dried orange peel
450ml (16floz/2 cups) peanut oil
*30g (1¼oz) fermented, salted soya
    beans*
1 tsp chopped garlic
75g (3oz) shallots
2 tsp rice wine

Seasonings
3 tbsp stock
1 tsp salt
*1 tsp monosodium glutamate
    (optional)*
1 tsp sugar
2 tsp dark soy sauce
*1 tbsp cornflour blended with 3
    tbsp water*

粟
米
魚
茸
羹

Chop the chicken into large, bite-size pieces and dust with corn-flour.

Cut the peppers and chillies into slices, and soak the dried orange peel before shredding it.

Heat the pan until it is very hot. Pour in the peanut oil and fry the chicken until it starts to turn brown.

Heat a clay pot or casserole until it is very hot. Pour 2 tbsp peanut oil into it and add the chillies, peppers, fermented beans, chopped garlic and shallots to sauté, stirring them together until fragrant.

Add the chicken pieces and sprinkle with rice wine. Sauté for a further 30 seconds.

Blend the seasonings and add to the pot. Stir and cover the container to cook for $1\frac{1}{2}$ minutes over a high heat. Keep the container covered until ready to serve.

CHICKEN, BAMBOO SHOOTS AND BLACK MUSHROOM CASSEROLE

600g (1½lb) chicken

Seasoning
2 tsp salt
1 tsp sesame oil
½ tsp pepper
2 tsp Chinese yellow wine or dry sherry
1 tbsp cornflour

6-8 medium black mushrooms
450ml (16floz/2 cups) peanut oil
100g (4oz) bamboo shoots, sliced
4 slices ginger

1 scallion, cut into 5cm (2in) lengths

Sauce
1 tbsp oyster sauce
1 tbsp soy sauce
1 tsp sugar
4 tbsp chicken broth

1 tsp sesame oil
1 tsp Chinese yellow wine
1 tbsp cornflour blended with 2 tbsp water

Cut the chicken into bite-size pieces. Mix the seasonings together thoroughly and add the chicken pieces. Mix and set aside.

Soak the black mushrooms in warm water for 30 minutes until they are soft; remove the stems.

Heat the oil and deep fry the chicken for $1\frac{1}{2}$ minutes over a moderate heat. Drain thoroughly.

Heat 2 tbsp oil in a casserole, add the mushrooms, bamboo shoots, ginger, scallion and the chicken and stir-fry over a high heat for $1\frac{1}{4}$ minutes.

Blend the sauce ingredients and add the mixture to the casserole. Bring to the boil and simmer for 15 minutes over a moderate to low heat.

Finally, add the sesame oil, yellow wine and blended cornflour, stir well and serve in the casserole.

鮮
人
參
雞

CHICKEN, BAMBOO SHOOTS
AND BLACK MUSHROOM
CASSEROLE
In spite of its exotic
name, this is a simple,
tasty casserole cooked the
Chinese way.

DOUBLE-BOILED FRESH
GINSENG FROM LIAONING
PROVINCE AND CHICKEN SOUP
The mysterious root
renowned for its
health-giving properties is
here used to make a
warming soup ideal for
winter nights.

粟米魚羹

QUICKLY BRAISED CHICKEN
WITH CHILLIES, GREEN PEPPERS
AND BLACK BEANS
A rich and very tasty dish
distinguished by the
unique taste of black
beans.

CHICKEN, ABALONE, BLACK
MUSHROOMS AND BAMBOO
SHOOTS IN A CLAY POT
This casserole is lifted
into the luxury class by
the addition of abalone,
which has a strong and
distinctive flavour.

DOUBLE-BOILED FRESH GINSENG FROM LIAONING PROVINCE AND CHICKEN SOUP

1kg (2-2¼lb) chicken
900ml (32floz/4 cups) boiling
  water
40g (1½oz) ham

500g (1¼lb) lean pork
1 fresh ginseng (approximately
  25g/1oz)

Clean the chicken and blanch it in the boiling water for 3 minutes together with the ham and lean pork.

Drain the meat and put it with the ginseng in a heavy pot or casserole with a lid. Add just enough hot water to cover and steam for 4 hours over medium heat.

Serve by bringing the pot or casserole to the table. The chicken and pork should be sufficiently tender to allow diners to take pieces of meat with their chopsticks. Season to taste.

ROAST GOOSE

1 young goose (approximately
  3kg/6lb)
1 tbsp soya bean paste
1 tsp five-spice powder
1 piece star anise
1 tbsp sugar
2 tbsp light soy sauce
2 tsp chopped garlic

1 tbsp Chinese yellow wine
1.25l (48floz/6 cups) boiling
  water
2 tbsp malt sugar
4 tbsp honey or corn syrup
4 tbsp vinegar
225ml (8floz/1 cup) water

Cut off the feet and wing tips of the goose. (If a young goose is not available, use a duck.)

Blend together the soya bean paste, five-spice powder, star anise, sugar, soy sauce, chopped garlic and yellow wine and rub the mixture all over the inside of the goose. Tightly fasten the neck and tail openings with skewers or string to ensure that the mixture does not run out when the goose is hung.

Place the goose on a rack, breast up, and pour half the boiling water over it. Turn the goose over and pour the remaining boiling water over it. Pat the goose dry and set it aside.

Heat the malt sugar, honey, vinegar and 225ml (8floz/1 cup) water together, stirring to mix well, and brush the mixture all over the goose.

Tie a piece of string around the neck of the goose and hang it up in a draughty place for 1 hour to dry.

Pre-heat the oven to 230°C (450°F/Gas Mark 8). Place the goose on a rack in a deep (5cm/2in) roasting pan and roast the goose, breast side up, for 12 minutes until golden. Turn the goose over with a towel (avoid using a fork) and roast for another 12 minutes.

Reduce the heat to 180°C (350°F/Gas Mark 4) and, with the goose breast side up again, roast for 20 minutes. Reduce the heat to 150°C (300°F/Gas Mark 2) and roast for a further 10 minutes, then reduce the heat to 130°C (250°F/Gas Mark ½) and roast for a further 10 minutes. Finally, increase the heat to 230°C (450°F/Gas Mark 8) again and roast for 10 minutes. You have to watch closely at this point to avoid burning the goose.

You may either chop the goose into bite-size pieces and serve with a plum jam, or serve the crispy skin first, as with Peking Duck, and use the remaining meat to make two more dishes, Roast Goose Casserole with Bamboo Shoots (page 61) and Stir-fried Minced Goose with Lettuce (below).

STIR-FRIED MINCED GOOSE WITH LETTUCE

4 medium Chinese dried mushrooms	¼ tsp pepper
450g (1lb) roast goose meat	1 tbsp light soy sauce
100g (4oz) bamboo shoots	½ tbsp yellow bean paste
2 garlic cloves	½ tbsp hoisin sauce
2 slices root-ginger	½ tbsp sugar
4 water chestnuts	1 tbsp Shaohsing rice wine or dry
1 stalk spring onion	sherry
4 tbsp peanut oil	1½ tsp sesame oil
1 tsp salt	2 sprigs of parsley to garnish
	12 lettuce leaves

Soak the mushrooms in hot water for 30 minutes. Remove and discard the stems and coarsely mince the caps. Chop the goose meat, bamboo shoots, garlic, ginger, water chestnuts and spring onion into a similar coarse mince.

Heat the oil in a pan or wok. When the oil is hot, add the ginger and mushrooms. Stir them in the hot oil for 30 seconds before adding the bamboo shoots, garlic and water chestnuts. Continue to stir and fry for 1 minute, then add the spring onion and goose meat, together with the salt and pepper. Continue to stir all the ingredients for 2 minutes, turning them over to ensure that they are all thoroughly cooked.

Sprinkle the soy sauce, yellow bean paste, hoisin sauce, sugar and rice wine over the pan, and continue to stir, turn and fry, over a medium heat, for 3 minutes. Add the sesame oil and serve, garnished with sprigs of parsley.

Diners help themselves to a couple of spoonfuls of the minced goose mixture. They place the mixture on a lettuce leaf, wrap it up carefully and eat it with their fingers.

STIR-FRIED MINCED GOOSE

STIR-FRIED MINCED GOOSE
WITH LETTUCE
The use of lettuce leaves
to wrap up minced
poultry is very much a
Hong Kong innovation.
Traditionally, the
wrapping would have
been of pancake — but
this is now regarded as
altogether too heavy and
filling when presented as
a part of a Chinese dinner
which may consist of
more than a dozen dishes.
This dish is often
reproduced using chicken
or pigeon.

ROAST GOOSE
Although roast duck is
better known as a
Chinese dish, roast goose
is actually preferred by
Cantonese gourmets.

FRIED CRISPY PIGEON
The crispy skin is easy enough to achieve, but striking the right balance of herbs and spices to flavour the broth is a delicate skill.

脆皮乳鴿

瑤
柱
火
鴨

ROAST DUCK WITH GARLIC

5-6 dried scallops
75g (3oz) of garlic
250g (9oz) roast duck breast
150 g (5oz) spinach
½ tsp salt
2 tbsp oil

Seasonings
1 tbsp soy sauce
¾ tsp sugar
1 tbsp oyster sauce
few drops sesame oil
1 tsp cornflour
2 tsp rice wine

Soak the scallops for 3-4 hours and steam for 30 minutes. Fry the garlic until brown.

Cut the duck breast into 12 slices (each slice with skin attached) and arrange the meat in a big bowl (the skin to the bottom of the bowl), add a layer of scallops and finally the garlic. Steam for 45 minutes.

Fry the spinach with a little salt and oil and spread it out on a plate. Put the roast duck, scallops and garlic on top of the spinach and reserve the gravy.

Boil the gravy from the bottom of the bowl in a pan. Add the seasonings and stir into a sauce. Pour the sauce over the dish and serve.

FRIED CRISPY PIGEON

2 young pigeons

Spicy stock
½ Chinese dried orange peel
2 star anise
1 tsp peppercorns
3 slices ginger
1 spring onion
2 tbsp dark soy sauce
1 tsp salt

1 tbsp sugar
1l (40floz/5 cups) water

½ tsp white vinegar
2 tsp malt sugar, molasses or honey
1 tsp cornflour
2 tsp water

450ml (16floz/2 cups) peanut oil

Clean the pigeons.

Prepare the ingredients for the spicy stock. Bring the mixture to the boil. Reduce the temperature and put the pigeons into the stock to simmer for 7 minutes. Remove and drain the pigeons and pat them dry.

Mix the vinegar, malt sugar and cornflour with 2 tsp of water and rub the pigeons with the mixture. Hang the pigeons up to dry for 3-4 hours.

Heat the oil and fry the pigeons, turning them from side to side

脆
皮
乳
鴿

and basting them with the hot oil all the time to fry them evenly until the pigeons become brown, which takes about 5 minutes. Remove the pigeons and drain. Chop the pigeon in bite-size pieces to serve.

PIGEONS IN DARK SOY SAUCE

2 pigeons
1l (40floz/5 cups) water
1 piece cinnamon stalk
2-3 slices liquorice root
3 slices ginger
4 shallots

225ml (8floz/1 cup) dark soy
  sauce
170ml (6floz/³/₄ cup) soy sauce
450ml (16floz/2 cups) stock
2 tbsp Chinese yellow wine
25g (1oz) rock sugar

Clean the pigeons. Boil 1l (40floz/5 cups) water and blanch the pigeons for 2 minutes. Remove the pigeons from the boiling water, drain and pat dry.

Place all the remaining ingredients in a clay pot and bring to the boil. Allow to simmer over a low heat for 15 minutes before putting the pigeons into the pot to simmer in the sauce for a further 15 minutes. Let the pigeons colour evenly by turning them over from time to time.

Cover the pot and turn off the heat, leaving the contents to sit for 30 minutes.

Dismember the pigeons and serve with the sauce from the cooking pot.

STIR-FRIED SUPREME OF PIGEON, BLACK MUSHROOMS AND BAMBOO SHOOTS

150g (5oz) supreme of pigeon
  (breast meat)

Marinade
1 tsp light soy sauce
¹/₂ tsp salt
¹/₂ tsp sesame oil
¹/₄ tsp pepper
1 tsp Chinese yellow wine
1 tbsp cornflour

5-6 medium black mushrooms
150g (5oz) bamboo shoots
450ml (16floz/2 cups) peanut oil

1 tsp salt
1 tbsp stock
¹/₂ tsp minced garlic
¹/₂ tsp minced ginger

Sauce
1 tbsp oyster sauce
1 tsp dark soy sauce
1 tbsp light soy sauce
2 tbsp stock
1 tsp sugar
¹/₂ tsp sesame oil
1 tbsp cornflour
1 tsp Chinese yellow wine

(Recipe continued on page 76)

瑤柱火鴨

ROAST DUCK WITH GARLIC
A good way to deal with
left-over roast duck is to
steam it until it is very
tender, adding conpoy
(dried scallops) and
garlic for flavour.

STIR-FRIED SUPREME OF
PIGEON, BLACK MUSHROOMS
AND BAMBOO SHOOTS
Mushrooms and bamboo
shoots form a
combination that crops
up time and again in
Chinese cooking. Pigeon
is used to make a change
from chicken and is
cooked in similar ways.

豉油王乳鴿

PIGEONS IN DARK SOY SAUCE
Only the best pigeons are
used for this dish, which
depends on the natural
taste of the bird more
than on seasonings.

PIGEON AND SHARK'S FIN IN A
CLAY POT
An extravagant casserole
compared to other clay
pot dishes, but well worth
the expense.

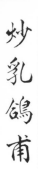

Cut the pigeon breasts into thin slices approximately 50 × 25 × 5mm (2 × 1 × ¼in). Mix together the marinade ingredients and marinate the pigeon slices. Set them on one side.

Soak the black mushrooms in hot water for about 30 minutes, remove and discard the stalks and cut the caps into thin slices. Cut the bamboo shoots into slices 30 × 20 × 4mm (1½ × ¾ × ¼in) thick.

Heat a pan until very hot, add the oil and after 1 minute add the pigeon pieces. Stir to separate. Remove them from the oil and set aside.

Reheat the pan and add the bamboo shoot and mushroom slices. Sauté for 1 minute. Add 1 tsp of salt and 1 tbsp stock, cook for 2 minutes and set aside.

Heat 2 tbsp oil in the pan. Add the garlic and ginger and when the fragrance arises add all the cooked ingredients. Stir-fry for 1 minute over high heat before adding the sauce ingredients. Stir rapidly for 15 seconds. Serve.

CHINESE CABBAGE, MUNG BEAN NOODLES, DRIED SHRIMPS AND SHREDDED PORK

500g (1¼lb) Chinese cabbage
100g (4oz) mung bean noodles
50g (2oz) dried shrimps
50g (2oz) fillet of pork

Seasoning
1 tsp salt
2 tsp cornflour
½ tsp sesame oil

½ tsp sugar

3-4 tbsp peanut oil
3-4 slices ginger
900ml (32floz/4 cups) chicken stock
1 tsp salt
2 tsp Chinese yellow wine

Cut the Chinese cabbage into 1 × 5cm (½ × 2in) pieces. Soak the mung bean noodles and the dried shrimps in water for about 15 minutes until they are softened.

Shred the fillet of pork and mix the meat with the seasoning ingredients.

Heat 3-4 tbsp oil in a clay pot or a wok and add the ginger slices and shredded fillet of pork, stirring to separate. Then add the dried shrimps.

Add the Chinese cabbage, stir and mix well. Pour in the chicken stock and bring the contents to the boil. Reduce the heat and simmer for 15 minutes. Add the mung bean noodles and simmer for a further 2-3 minutes. Finally add salt and Chinese yellow wine and serve.

This simple recipe nevertheless has marvellous flavour. If you increase the quantities of chicken stock and wine, the dish becomes more soup-like in consistency. Either way, it should be served with a bowl of rice.

乳
鴿
吞
翅

PIGEON AND SHARK'S FIN IN A CLAY POT

100g (4oz) soaked tiger shark's fin
1 king pigeon (approximately
    500g/1¼lb)
25g (1oz) cooked ham, shredded
450ml (16floz/2 cups) peanut oil
    (to fry pigeon)
3 pieces sliced ginger
2 stalks spring onions
2 mushrooms

50g (2oz) roast pork
½l (20floz/3 cups) unsalted stock

Seasonings
1½ tsp salt
½ tsp monosodium glutamate
1 tsp sugar
1 tbsp oyster sauce

Soak the shark's fin in water overnight. Drain thoroughly.

Clean the pigeon and blanch it in boiling water for 1 minute. Drain thoroughly. Break up the shark's fin and insert the pieces and the shredded ham into the cavity of the pigeon. Close the cavity with a skewer.

Bring the peanut oil to high heat, add the pigeon and fry until the bird turns brown. Drain well.

Heat the clay pot, and pour 2 tbsp peanut oil into it. Add the ginger, spring onions, mushrooms and roast pork to sauté until fragrant (about 2 minutes). Add the pigeon, unsalted stock and the seasonings, and stew gently for 2½ hours. Serve in the clay pot.

DOUBLE-BOILED PIGEON, HAM AND BLACK MUSHROOM SOUP

2 pigeons
225g (8oz) lean pork
6 medium black mushrooms
40g (1½oz) ham

3 slices ginger
1 tbsp Chinese yellow wine
½l (20floz/3 cups) chicken stock
2-3 tbsp oil

Clean the pigeons thoroughly. Cut out the breast meat and save it for a Stir-fried Supreme of Pigeon.

Blanch the lean pork and pigeons in boiling water for 2 minutes and rinse under the tap for 1 minute.

Soak the black mushrooms in warm water for about 30 minutes until they have softened. Discard the stems and cut the caps into evenly sized pieces.

Put all ingredients in a heavy pot or casserole with a lid, add the stock and an equal amount of water, and cover and steam over medium heat for 3 hours.

(Double boiling is the favourite Cantonese way of preparing soup. The Cantonese believe that it not only makes the flavour richer but increases the nutritional value.)

SALT-BAKED PIGEON

鹽
焗
乳
鴿

SALT-BAKED PIGEON
This is a variant on the more usual Cantonese salt-baked chicken. The salt crust serves to seal in the flavour of the meat while making the outside deliciously crispy.

CHINESE CABBAGE, MUNG BEAN NOODLES, DRIED SHRIMPS AND SHREDDED PORK
An inexpensive, homely dish with a semi-soup consistency. Dried shrimps — stronger in flavour than fresh — are used in China like stock cubes in the west, to provide a savoury base. More than half the liquid is absorbed by the transparent mung bean noodles (known in the U.S. as cellophane noodles).

清湯伊麵

E-FU NOODLES IN SOUP
Adding shredded pork to
the soup makes it a
complete meal, but the
soup is delicious by itself
or as part of a meal.

**DOUBLE-BOILED PIGEON, HAM
AND BLACK MUSHROOM SOUP**
The basic savouriness of
this dish comes from the
pigeon; the ham and
mushrooms vary the
flavour. Double-boiling,
or slow steaming in a
closed pot, is an
alternative to boiling.

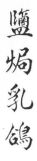

鹽
焗
乳
鴿

SALT-BAKED PIGEON

2 pigeons	1 tsp Chinese yellow wine
	1 tbsp dark soy sauce
Marinade	1 tsp ginger juice
1 crushed star anise	
2 shallot cloves	1/2 tsp sesame oil
1 tbsp shredded spring onion	2 1/2 kg (5-6lb) coarse salt
1 tsp shredded ginger	2 sheets greaseproof paper
2 slices liquorice root	2 sheets foil

Clean the pigeons and dry them with a paper towel. Mix together the star anise, shallots, spring onion, ginger and liquorice and rub the skin and the inside of the pigeons with the mixture.

Blend the yellow wine, soy sauce, ginger juice and sesame oil together, divide it and put it into the cavities of the pigeons.

Stir-fry the coarse salt over high heat for 2 minutes. Insert about one-third of the salt into the pigeon cavities, and cover the outside of the birds with the remaining salt.

Wrap each pigeon first with a piece of greaseproof paper and then with foil. Bake the wrapped pigeons in an oven at 180°C (350°F/Gas Mark 4) for 40 minutes.

Remove the paper and foil from the pigeons and shake them free of salt. To serve, cut the pigeons into bite-size pieces.

E-FU NOODLES IN SOUP

2l (4 pints/10 cups) water	1/2 l (20fl oz/3 cups) chicken stock
2 cakes E-Fu noodles	1 tbsp light soy sauce
2 tbsp peanut oil	1 tsp sesame oil
2-3 slices ginger	25g (1oz) ham, finely shredded
250g (9oz) bean sprouts	50g (2oz) Chinese white chives, cut
1/2 tsp salt	into 4cm (1 3/4 in) lengths

Bring the water to the boil and blanch the E-Fu noodles for 2 minutes. Remove them from the water, drain, press with a towel and set aside.

Heat the oil in a pan and add the ginger slices. Remove and discard the ginger when it has browned and add the bean sprouts. Stirring, cook over a very high heat for 30 seconds, then add the salt, continuing to stir, and cook for 10 more seconds. Remove the ingredients from the oil and set them aside.

Heat the chicken stock in a pot, add the noodles and cook for 30 seconds. Add the soy sauce and sesame oil.

Transfer to a soup tureen and sprinkle the shredded ham on

top. Add the bean sprouts and white chives and serve.

This soup makes an appetizing snack or it can be served with other dishes as part of a meal. If you add shredded pork, it becomes a complete meal by itself.

BRAISED E-FU NOODLES WITH SHREDDED PORK AND MUSHROOMS

Sauce
1 tbsp oyster sauce
1 tbsp light soy sauce
1 tsp dark soy sauce
1 tsp sesame oil
½ tsp sugar

50g (2oz) fillet of pork

1 tsp cornflour
2 medium black mushrooms
100g (4oz) chives
900ml (32floz/4 cups) boiling
   water
350g (12oz) E-Fu noodles
3-4 tbsp peanut oil
1 tbsp shredded ginger

Mix the sauce ingredients together in a bowl. Cut the fillet of pork into matchstick-size shreds and add 1 tbsp of the mixed sauce and 1 tsp of cornfour. Mix well and set aside.

Soak the black mushrooms in hot water for 30 minutes. Remove and discard the stems and cut the caps into shreds. Set aside. Cut the chives into 3cm (1½in) pieces and set aside. Bring the water to the boil and add the E-Fu noodles. Parboil until soft. Remove, drain and dry the noodles with paper towels.

Heat 3-4 tbsp oil in a pan. Add the shredded ginger and fillet of pork and stir-fry for 1 minute. Add the mushrooms, stir and continue to cook for a further minute. Return the E-Fu noodles to the pan and add the remainder of the sauce. Stir and mix the ingredients together, simmering over medium heat until all water is absorbed by the noodles.

Sprinkle the chives over the noodles and cook for 30 seconds. Transfer to a plate and serve immediately.

SPARE RIBS WITH ORANGE

450g (1lb) spare ribs

Marinade
½ tsp salt
½ tsp sugar
¼ tsp monosodium glutamate
   (optional)
2 tsp ginger juice
1 tbsp cornflour

few drops of sesame oil

450ml (16floz/2 cups) peanut oil
1 tbsp cointreau
4 tbsp orange juice
2 tsp cornflour
½ tsp monosodium glutamate
   (optional)
half an orange

(Recipe continued on page 84)

梅子鯉魚煲

SPARE RIBS WITH ORANGE
The fruity flavour goes
marvellously with the
spare rib: a really
delicious recipe.

蠔皇牛肉

BEEF WITH OYSTER SAUCE
This dish is a commonplace in Chinese restaurants everywhere — but, if you follow this recipe carefully, you will produce the dish at its very best.

BRAISED E-FU NOODLES WITH SHREDDED PORK AND MUSHROOMS
Once the pork has been stewed by the usual red cooking method, the gravy, with added mushrooms, is used to braise the E-Fu noodles.

Chop the spare ribs into portions 5cm (2in) long. Prepare the marinade mix and use it to marinate the ribs for 1 hour.

Heat the peanut oil. Fry the spare ribs for 1 minute. Remove from heat but keep the ribs in the oil for 3 minutes, then remove them. Reheat the oil and return the ribs for another minute. Remove the ribs and drain away the oil.

Heat the pan and pour in 1 tbsp oil. Mix together the cointreau, orange juice, 2 tsp cornflour and the monosodium glutamate (if used), and add the mixture to the pan and bring to the boil.

Add the ribs to the pan and cook over a high heat for 10 seconds. Garnish with orange slices and serve.

The fruity flavour of the orange goes marvellously with the spare rib in this delicious recipe.

STIR-FRIED SHREDDED FILLET OF BEEF IN A BIRD'S NEST

Marinade
$^1/_2$ tsp sugar
1 tsp dry sherry or Shaohsing wine
2 tsp cornflour
$^1/_4$ tsp sesame oil
1 tbsp soy sauce

175g (6oz) fillet of beef, shredded
2 potatoes, finely shredded
450ml (16fl oz/2 cups) peanut oil

Sauce
$^1/_2$ tsp salt

$^1/_2$ tsp monosodium glutamate (optional)
$^1/_2$ tsp sugar
$2^1/_2$ tsp oyster sauce
2 tbsp water

1 garlic clove, chopped
100g (4oz) pickled cabbage or bamboo shoot
1 red chilli
1 green pepper
1 tbsp flour
$^1/_2$ tsp salt

Prepare the marinade, omitting the soy sauce, and steep the shredded fillet of beef for 20 minutes. Just before cooking, add the soy sauce and mix well.

To make the bird's nest, lay potato shreds in a large, perforated metal spoon or ladle, making a bowl shape by pressing the shredded potato down with another spoon. Deep fry in the perforated spoon until golden brown and crisp. Arrange on a dish.

Heat 450ml (16fl oz/2 cups) oil in a pan. Add the beef and stir to separate. Turn the heat off as soon as beef changes colour. Remove the beef and drain.

Mix the sauce ingredients and set aside.

Put 1 tbsp oil in a pan. When it is hot, stir-fry the garlic first, then add the pickled cabbage or bamboo shoots, red chilli and green pepper (all shredded) and continue to fry for 1 minute.

Add the shredded beef and mixed sauce and stir-fry all the ingredients together for 30 seconds. Serve in the bird's nest.

蠔
皇
牛
肉

BEEF WITH OYSTER SAUCE

300g (11oz) beef steak
25g (1oz) ginger
75g (3oz) white part of spring
    onions

Marinade
1½ tsp ginger juice
1½ tsp rice wine
2 tsp soy sauce
½ tsp sugar
1 egg white
½ tsp meat tenderizer (optional)
1 tbsp oil

1 tbsp cornflour

450ml (16floz/2 cups) oil (for
    frying beef)
1 tsp chopped garlic
2 tsp rice wine

Sauce
1½ tbsp oyster sauce
1 tsp soy sauce
3 tbsp stock or water
1 tsp cornflour

Cut the beef into very thin slices, 3 × 2cm (1½ × ¾in). Slice the ginger and cut the spring onions into pieces 4-5cm (2in) long. Mix the marinade ingredients and marinate the beef for 1 hour.

Heat a pan over high heat and add the oil, reducing to a low heat when the oil is hot. Add the beef and fry for 30 seconds. Remove with a perforated spoon and allow to drain.

Fry the ginger and spring onions for a short while and remove.

Heat the pan again over high heat. Add 2 tbsp oil and fry the garlic, ginger and spring onions for 15 seconds. Add the beef and sprinkle with rice wine.

Mix the sauce ingredients and add to the pan. Stir-fry for 30 seconds over a high heat. Serve, fresh and hot from the pan.

STEWED BRISKET OF BEEF WITH TURNIPS

1kg (2lb) brisket of beef
1kg (2lb) turnips
6 tbsp peanut oil
2 star anise
1 tsp peppercorns
50g (2oz) ginger slices
2-3 garlic cloves
2 tbsp soy bean paste

Sauce
1 tbsp oyster sauce
2 tsp dark soy sauce
2 tbsp light soy sauce
2 tbsp cornflour
1 tbsp Chinese yellow wine
1 tsp sugar

Blanch the brisket of beef in 1l (40fl oz//5 cups) boiling water for 5 minutes. Remove from the water, cut into 3cm (1½ in) cubes.

Peel the turnips, and cut them into 5cm (2in) wedges. Cook them in ½l (20fl oz/3 cups) boiling water for 15 minutes stirring all the time. Set aside.

Heat a pan over high heat and add 2 tbsp oil. When the oil is hot, add the beef, star anise and peppercorns and cook for 3-5

鵲
巢
牛
柳

STIR-FRIED SHREDDED FILLET
OF BEEF IN A BIRD'S NEST
The 'bird's nest' is made
of crispy shreds of potato,
which form a basket for
the meat. The soft texture
of the stir-fried beef
contrasts well with the
crackliness of the potato.

鵲
巢
牛
柳

鵲巢牛柳

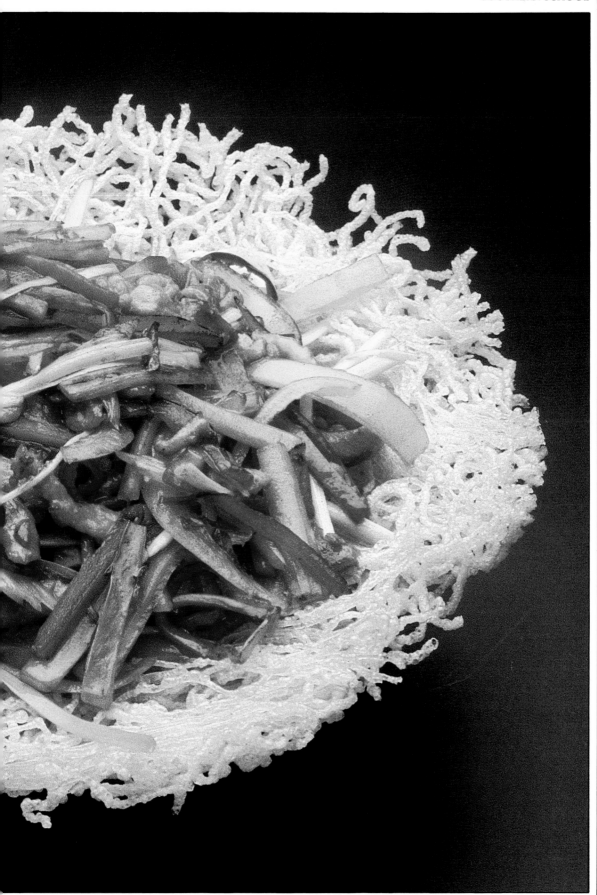

紅
炆
牛
腩

minutes, stirring all the time. Set aside.

Heat 4 tbsp oil in a clay pot, heavy saucepan or casserole. Add the ginger, garlic and soy bean paste and, when the aroma rises, add the beef and cook, stirring, for 1 minute over very high heat.

Add enough water to well cover the meat. Bring to the boil, lower the heat and simmer for 1 hour. Turn off the heat and allow to stand for 1 hour.

Bring to the boil again and simmer for 30 minutes. Add the turnips and sauce ingredients. Mix well and simmer for 15 minutes before serving.

STIR-FRIED SLICED BEEF, SQUID, FRESH MUSHROOM AND BABY CORN

150g (5oz) fillet of beef
150g (5oz) squid
200g (7oz) straw mushrooms, fresh or tinned
200g (7oz) baby corn

Seasoning for beef
2 tsp light soy sauce
1/2 tsp sesame oil
1/2 tsp pepper
1/2 tsp sugar
1 tbsp cornflour

Seasoning for squid
1 tsp ginger juice
1 tsp Chinese yellow wine
1/2 tsp salt
1/2 tsp sesame oil
1 tbsp cornflour

225ml (8fl oz/1 cup) peanut oil

1 tsp salt
1/2 tsp minced garlic
3-4 slices ginger
2-3 slices spring onion cut into 3cm (1 1/2in) lengths
1 1/2 tbsp Chinese yellow wine

Sauce
2 tsp oyster sauce
1/2 tsp monosodium glutamate (optional)
2 tsp soy sauce
1/2 tsp salt
1 tsp sugar
1/4 tsp pepper
1 tbsp cornflour
6 tbsp stock
few drops sesame oil
1 tsp Chinese yellow wine
4 tbsp peanut oil

Cut the fillet of beef into very thin slices 5 × 7cm (2 × 3in).

Divide the squid into pieces 2 × 5cm (³/₄ × 2in), scoring the flesh on one side to form a diamond pattern. Cut the straw mushrooms and baby corns into halves.

Separately prepare the individual seasonings for the beef and the squid. Heat a pan, add 225ml (8fl oz/1 cup) oil and heat for 1 minute over medium heat. Add the seasoned beef, stir to separate and remove with a perforated spoon after 75 seconds.

Add the seasoned squid to the oil, removing it with a strainer when it curls up.

Keep 1 tbsp oil in the pan. Add the baby corns, straw mushrooms, 1 tsp salt and stir well over a high heat for 30 seconds. Remove and set aside.

海陸雙珍

Heat the pan, this time over a very high heat and add 2 tbsp oil, the minced garlic and ginger slices. When the aroma arises, add the beef, squid and spring onions, sprinkle 1 tbsp Chinese yellow wine over them and stir rapidly for 30 seconds. Add the baby corns and straw mushrooms. Stir for 30 seconds.

Blend together the sauce ingredients and add them to the pan. Stir for 10 seconds, sprinkle with ½ tbsp of wine and serve.

STIR-FRIED SHREDDED BEEF WITH PICKLED MUSTARD GREEN, GREEN PEPPER AND RED CHILLIES

Marinade
½ egg white
1 tsp cornflour
½ tsp sesame oil
1 tsp Chinese yellow wine
1 tbsp light soy sauce
½ tsp sugar

300g (11oz) fillet of beef
300g (11oz) pickled mustard green
300g (11oz) green pepper
2 red chillies
2 tsp sugar
3 tbsp peanut oil

1 tsp salt
225ml (8fl oz/1 cup) peanut oil
25g (1oz) rice vermicelli
1 tsp chopped ginger
1 tsp chopped garlic

Sauce
1 tbsp oyster sauce
1 tbsp light soy sauce
1 tsp dark soy sauce
1 tsp sesame oil
1 tsp sugar
1 tbsp cornflour
8 tbsp chicken stock

Prepare the marinade ingredients in a separate bowl. Cut the fillet of beef into matchstick-size shreds and marinate. Set aside.

Soak the pickled mustard green in water for 30 minutes. Chop into shreds and set aside. Shred the green pepper and red chilli into 'double matchstick-size' pieces.

Heat a pan and add the chopped pickled mustard green, stirring to cook over a medium heat until quite dry. Add 2 tsp sugar and 1 tbsp oil, stir and cook for 30 seconds. Remove and set aside.

Heat 1 tbsp oil in the pan and add the green pepper and 1 tsp salt. Stir-fry for 2 minutes. Remove and set aside.

Heat 225ml (8fl oz/1 cup) oil in a pan and add the beef, stirring to separate. Remove with a perforated spoon and set aside.

Heat the same oil for 15 seconds and add the rice vermicelli. It should expand and froth up immediately. Remove straight away and put on a plate to keep warm.

Heat 1 tbsp oil. Add the chopped ginger, garlic and red chillies and, when the aroma rises, return the beef, pickled mustard green and green pepper to the pan. Blend and add the sauce ingredients. Stir-fry over very high heat for 1 minute, place on top of the crispy rice vermicelli on the serving dish and serve.

酸
菜
牛
柳
絲

STIR-FRIED SHREDDED BEEF
WITH PICKLED MUSTARD
GREEN, GREEN PEPPER AND
RED CHILLIES

This is called a Cantonese
dish but it can also be a
Sichuan dish, depending
on the amount of chilli
used. The chilli is fried
briefly in oil so that the
hotness pervades the oil.
The same can be done
with the pickle. The
shredded beef and green
pepper are cooked only
briefly. Adding vinegar
enhances the fieriness of
the chilli, and as much as
a tablespoon of sugar
may be included in the
stir-fry. The whole dish
can be cooked in 4 or 5
minutes.

STIR-FRIED SLICED BEEF,
SQUID, FRESH MUSHROOM AND
BABY CORN

The success of this dish
depends on presenting
the four main ingredients
almost separately, so that
the different flavours,
colours and textures
remain distinct.

羊腩煲

BRAISED MUTTON IN A CLAY POT

A slow-cooked dish probably introduced to Canton from the north (Peking or Outer Mongolia), where mutton is more common. The meat is cooked in a simple way and is served with one or more stronger-tasting sauces for dipping into.

STEWED BRISKET OF BEEF WITH TURNIPS

Beef and turnip make up a traditional Chinese combination. Brisket has a good flavour because of the fat it contains. It is cooked for almost three hours and produces a very tasty gravy, which is poured over rice.

羊
腩
煲

BRAISED MUTTON IN A CLAY POT

1½kg (3lb) braising mutton (belly
    if possible)
4l (8 pints) water (for blanching
    mutton)
75g (3oz) bean curd sticks
75g (3oz) bamboo shoots
3-4 tbsp peanut oil
80g (3½oz) sliced ginger
80g (3½oz) leeks, cut into 3cm
    (1½in) pieces
40g (1½oz) salted fermented soya
    bean paste
3 tbsp Chinese yellow wine
2l (4 pints) water (for braising
    mutton)
6-8 Chinese dried mushrooms

80g (3½oz) oyster sauce
50g (2oz) whole dried orange peel
75g (3oz) water chestnuts
100g (4oz) sugar-cane
3 lemon leaves

3 tbsp oyster sauce
1 tsp salt

Dip
3 tbsp fermented bean curd or
    bean curd 'cheese'
shredded lemon leaves
gravy from mutton in clay pot –
    about 6 tbsp, enough to make
    one or two small dishes of dip

Blanch the mutton in 4l (8 pints) water over a high heat for 10 minutes. Remove the mutton and chop it into large, bite-size pieces.

Soak the bean curd sticks in water for 1 hour. Fry the bamboo shoots for a short while until they turn bright yellow, which indicates that the water has been extracted from the shoots.

Heat the pan until it is very hot and pour 3-4 tbsp oil to the pan. Add the ginger, leeks and soya bean paste into the hot oil to release their aromatic flavours. Then add the mutton and pour in the Chinese yellow wine. Stir and turn for 10 minutes.

Transfer the ingredients from the pan to a clay pot. Add all the remaining ingredients and 2l (4 pints) of water. Simmer the mutton for 1 hour over medium heat. Remove the sugar-cane and lemon leaves and add the oyster sauce and salt to taste.

Mix the ingredients for the dip. The mutton is served with the dip, each piece of meat being dipped into the sauce before being eaten. The sauce or soup is excellent with rice.

BRAISED BEAN CURD IN SHRIMP ROE SAUCE WITH CHINESE FLOWERING CABBAGE

6 squares bean curd
1kg (2lb) Chinese green flowering
    cabbage
450ml (16floz/2 cups) plus 2 tbsp
    peanut oil
1 tsp chopped ginger
1 tsp chopped garlic
1 tbsp shrimp roe

1 tbsp oyster sauce
1 tbsp light soy sauce
2 tsp Chinese yellow wine
1 tbsp cornflour
4 tbsp chicken stock
1 tsp salt
1 tsp dark soy sauce
1 tsp sesame oil

紅燒豆腐

Cut each square of bean curd into four pieces.

Remove the outer leaves of the Chinese flowering cabbage and blanch the heart for 3 minutes in 450ml (16fl oz/2 cups) boiling, salted water with 2 tbsp oil added. Remove the cabbage and set it aside keeping it warm.

Heat 450ml (16fl oz/2 cup) oil in a pan. Add the pieces of bean curd and cook until they are nicely golden in colour. Remove them from the pan, drain and set them aside.

Heat 2 tbsp oil in the pan and add the ginger and garlic. When the aroma rises, add the shrimp roe, oyster sauce, light soy sauce, Chinese yellow wine, cornflour and stock, stir and cook for 30 seconds. Return the bean curd pieces to the pan and mix them thoroughly in the sauce.

Sprinkle the salt, dark soy sauce and sesame oil over the pan, stir and serve with the cabbage.

POACHED KIDNEY AND LIVER WITH SPRING ONION AND GINGER

225g (8oz) pig's kidney	**Sauce**
225g (8oz) pig's liver	8 tbsp chicken stock
4 tbsp peanut oil	2 tsp dark soy sauce
450ml (16fl oz/2 cups) boiling water	2 tbsp light soy sauce
1 tbsp salt	1 tsp sugar
2 tbsp shredded ginger	1 tsp sesame oil
4 tbsp shredded spring onion	2 tsp Chinese yellow wine

Slit open the kidney and remove the membrane and gristle. Cut the kidney into slices 3mm (⅛in) thick and soak in cold water. Set aside.

Cut the liver into slices 3mm (⅛in) thick. Soak in cold water and set aside.

Heat 2 tbsp oil in a pan, add the boiling water, bring to the boil and add the salt.

Add the kidney to the boiling water. Poach for 2 minutes, remove and drain.

Bring the water to the boil again and add the liver. Poach for 2 minutes, remove and drain.

Bring the water to the boil for the third time. Return the kidney and liver and add the shredded ginger and spring onion. Turn off the heat and allow the ingredients to stand in the hot water for 4-5 minutes. Remove and drain.

In the meantime prepare the sauce. Heat 2 tbsp oil in a pan, add the sauce ingredients and bring to the boil.

Transfer the poached kidney, liver, ginger and spring onion to a serving dish, pour the sauce on top and serve.

白灼腰膶

POACHED KIDNEY AND LIVER
WITH SPRING ONION AND
GINGER
The use of spring onion
and ginger in this dish
makes the taste of the
offal meats more
acceptable. The kidney is
poached only for a short
time and should still be
slightly crunchy.

STIR-FRIED ASSORTED MEATS
WITH THIN RICE-FLOUR
NOODLES IN CURRY SAUCE
Sometimes called
Singapore noodles, this
dish shows the influence
of the south in the use of
rice, rather than wheat,
noodles and in the curry
flavouring. It is important
to release the flavour of
the curry by frying it with
the meat or with garlic or
ginger before adding
stock or sauce.

紅燒豆腐

STIR-FRIED SHREDDED LAMB, BAMBOO SHOOTS, BLACK MUSHROOMS AND GREEN PEPPER ON CRISPY FRIED RICE NOODLES
Here the flavour of the north, in the form of lamb, is combined with the texture of the south, in the form of rice noodles fried until they are almost as crispy as a bird's nest.

BRAISED BEAN CURD IN SHRIMP ROE SAUCE WITH CHINESE FLOWERING CABBAGE
Bean curd tastes very bland unless cooked with strongly flavoured foods. Here shrimp roes provide the savoury taste.

STIR-FRIED SHREDDED LAMB, BAMBOO SHOOTS, BLACK MUSHROOMS AND GREEN PEPPER ON CRISPY FRIED RICE NOODLES

500g (1¼lb) fillet of lamb

Marinade
1 egg white
2 tsp cornflour
1 tbsp light soy sauce
1 tsp sugar
1 tsp Chinese yellow wine
1 tsp sesame oil

4 medium black mushrooms
300g (11oz) fresh bamboo shoots
1 green pepper
450ml (16floz/2 cups) peanut oil
25g (1oz) dried rice vermicelli

noodles
1½ tsp chopped garlic
1½ tsp chopped ginger

Sauce
1 tbsp oyster sauce
1 tbsp light soy sauce
½ tsp sugar
½ tsp sesame oil
1 tbsp Chinese yellow wine
½ cup chicken stock
1 tbsp cornflour

1 tbsp finely shredded lime leaves
1 tbsp chopped coriander

Shred the lamb into matchstick-size pieces and mix well with the marinade. Set aside.

Soak the black mushrooms in hot water for 30 minutes. Cut away and discard the stems and squeeze the mushrooms to remove any excess water. Shred the caps and set aside.

Finely chop the bamboo shoots and green pepper. Blanch the bamboo shoots in 900ml (32floz/4 cups) boiling water for 2 minutes. Remove and rinse under tap. Drain and set aside.

Heat the oil in a pan. Add the lamb and, after 75 seconds, stir to separate. Remove and set aside.

Add the dried rice noodles to the hot oil, removing them as soon as they fluff up (it takes only an instant). Place them as a bed on a large platter and keep warm.

Heat 3-4 tbsp oil in the pan and add the garlic and ginger. When the aroma arises, add the black mushrooms, green pepper and bamboo shoots and sauté for 1 minute. Return the lamb and stir rapidly over a very high heat for 30 seconds.

Add the sauce ingredients and continue to stir over a very high heat for another 30 seconds. Transfer to the platter and place on top of the noodles. Add the lime leaves and coriander and serve.

STIR-FRIED ASSORTED MEATS WITH THIN RICE-FLOUR NOODLES IN CURRY SAUCE

Marinade
1 tbsp egg white (from main recipe)

1 tsp salt
2 tsp cornflour
½ tsp sesame oil

星
洲
炒
米
粉

425g (15oz) dried rice-flour
    noodles (rice vermicelli)
2 eggs
100g (4oz) fillet of pork
100g (4oz) shrimps, shelled and
    deveined
1 green pepper
1 red chilli
7 tbsp peanut oil
1 tbsp chopped spring onion

Curry sauce
1 tbsp curry paste
1 tsp chopped garlic
1 tsp sugar
2 tbsp light soy sauce
170ml (6fl oz/¾ cup) chicken
    stock

1 tbsp chopped coriander

Soak the dried rice-flour noodles in 1.25l (48fl oz/6 cups) cold water for 15 minutes. Drain and set aside.

Break 2 eggs into a mixing bowl, taking 1 tbsp of egg white for the marinade. Beat the remainder lightly and set aside. Make the marinade in a separate bowl.

Cut the fillet of pork into matchstick-size shreds and mix with half of the marinade. Set aside.

Clean the shrimps, pat them dry and mix with the other half of the marinade. Keep refrigerated for 30 minutes.

Cut the green pepper and red chilli into thin shreds. Set aside.

Heat 2 tbsp oil. Stir-fry the chopped spring onions until nicely browned; remove and set aside. Add the shrimps and pork, stir-frying them for 1 minute. Remove and set aside.

Make the curry sauce by heating 1½ tbsp oil in a pan. Add the garlic and curry paste. When the aroma rises, add the sugar, soy sauce and chicken stock. Bring to the boil, transfer to a bowl and set aside.

Heat 3 tbsp oil in a pan until very hot. Add the rice noodles and stir, turning the noodles over with the help of chopsticks. Stir-fry over a high heat for 3 minutes. Transfer to a plate and set aside.

Add 1 tbsp oil to the pan. Fry the beaten egg until partially set and add the green pepper and red chilli. Keep stirring.

Return the shrimps and pork, and stir. Add the rice noodles to the pan and the curry sauce, stirring vigorously over a high heat for 3 minutes. Transfer to a plate, place the fried spring onion and chopped coriander on top and serve.

WONTON SOUP

40 wontons (see Deep-fried
    Wonton with Sweet-and-sour
    Sauce page 100; increase the
    quantities accordingly)
1¼ tbsp dried shrimps
1 tbsp peanut oil
4 slices ginger

900ml (32fl oz/4 cups) chicken
    stock
2 tsp sugar
2 tsp sesame oil
4-6 tsp light soy sauce
2 tbsp chopped spring onions

(Recipe continued on page 100)

呑
麵
油
菜

WONTON SOUP AND POACHED VEGETABLES WITH OYSTER SAUCE

Wonton soup (see also right) is very popular in Canton, where it is often served in tea houses to accompany *dimsum* (savoury snacks). Poaching need not be done in water — hot oil may be used instead. In the north seafood would be used for flavour. The Cantonese, however, use oyster sauce and perhaps a touch of seasame oil.

DEEP-FRIED WONTON

This is a favourite Chinese starter for a party dinner. Deep frying makes the wonton very crispy. Sweet-and-sour sauce is used for dipping or poured over the wonton.

錦鹵炸雲吞

Make and wrap the wontons.

Soak the dried shrimps in 225ml (8fl oz/1 cup) hot water for 30 minutes.

Heat 1 tbsp oil in a pot or casserole and add the ginger and dried shrimps, stirring until the aroma rises. Add the chicken stock plus the water used to soak the shrimps. Bring the contents to the boil, reduce the heat and simmer for 30 minutes. Add the sugar and keep warm in the pot.

Use four or six soup bowls and put into each ¼ tsp sesame oil, 1 tsp light soy sauce and 1 tsp chopped spring onion. Set aside.

Bring 2l (4 pints/20 cups) water to the boil. Add the wonton. Reduce the heat to medium and simmer for 5 minutes. Remove with a perforated spoon and divide them equally among the soup bowls. Add the soup and serve.

POACHED VEGETABLES WITH OYSTER SAUCE

1 kg (2lb) Chinese greens
  (flowering cabbage, Chinese
  spinach or lettuce)

3-4 tbsp peanut oil
3-4 tbsp oyster sauce

Clean the vegetables. If you are using Chinese greens or Chinese kale, remove and discard the flowers and tough woody stem.

Bring the water used to poach the wontons to the boil. Put in the vegetables and cook for 3-5 minutes (if you are using lettuce cook for only 1 minute). Remove and cut into 5cm (2in) pieces.

Place the vegetables on a plate, add boiling peanut oil and oyster sauce and serve.

Instead of oyster sauce I always use 1 tbsp of light and 1 tbsp of dark soy sauce and like the taste even more.

DEEP-FRIED WONTON ACCOMPANIED BY ASSORTED MEAT IN SWEET-AND-SOUR SAUCE

Filling
100g (4oz) fillet of pork
20g pork fat
20-30 shrimps, shelled and
  deveined
1 tsp salt
⅛ tsp pepper
1 tsp sesame oil

20-30 wonton wrappers
½ egg white
50g (2oz) cooked chicken meat

50g (2oz) roast duck meat
50g (2oz) cooked squid
1 medium onion
2-3 medium tomatoes
2 hard-boiled eggs
½l (20fl oz/3 cups) peanut oil
1 tsp chopped ginger
1 tsp chopped garlic
50g (2oz) cooked shrimps
340ml (12fl oz/1½ cups) sweet-
  and-sour sauce (see page 37)

錦
鹵
炸
雲
吞

This is an excellent recipe for injecting new life into leftovers.

Dice the fillet of pork and the pork fat into small pieces and mix thoroughly with the other ingredients for the filling.

Place 1 tsp filling in the centre of one wonton wrapper. Wet the opposite corners of the wrapper with egg white and gather the four corners of the wrapper together, squeezing them gently to form a small ball. Repeat the process until all the filling and wrappers are used. Set aside.

Cut the cooked chicken, roast duck and the squid into bite-sized pieces. Set aside. Cut the onion into wedges, pull the slices apart and set aside. Cut the tomatoes into wedges and each hard-boiled egg into four pieces.

Heat the oil until hot. Add the wonton and deep-fry for minute. Turn off the heat and let them cook in oil for 3 minutes before removing them. Increase the heat to bring the oil back to a high temperature again and fry the wonton for another minute. Remove, drain and transfer them to a serving dish.

Heat 2 tbsp oil in a pan. Add the ginger, garlic and onion and sauté for 1 minute. Add the chicken, roast duck, shrimps and squid and, stirring, cook for 30 seconds. Add the sweet-and-sour sauce.

The diners dip the crispy wonton into the sweet-and-sour sauce before eating them.

FRESH MUSHROOMS AND BAMBOO SHOOTS IN SHRIMP ROE SAUCE

400g (14oz) fresh straw
mushrooms
400g (14oz) bamboo shoots
225ml (8fl oz/1 cup) peanut oil
1 garlic clove
4 slices ginger
1 tbsp dried shrimp roe (if not
available use bottled shrimp
sauce)
1 tsp salt
1 tsp sugar

Sauce
1 tbsp oyster sauce
1 tbsp light soy sauce
1 tsp dark soy sauce
1/2 tsp sugar
1 tsp sesame oil
1 tsp Chinese yellow wine
1 1/2 tbsp cornflour
8 tbsp chicken stock

Cut the mushrooms in half, and cut the bamboo shoots into slices 20 × 40 × 2 mm (1 × 2 × 1/8 in).

Blanch the bamboo shoots in 450ml (16fl oz/2 cups) boiling water for 5 minutes. Remove and set aside. (If you are using tinned bamboo shoots this is not necessary.)

Blanch the mushrooms in boiling water for 1 minute. (Again, this is not necessary if you are using tinned mushrooms.) Remove and set aside.

七彩銀芽

COLOURFUL BEAN SPROUTS

The bright colours of the vegetables used in this dish give it great visual appeal. Bean sprouts are a handy vegetable because they grow easily indoors all year round and are pleasantly crunchy, but they can be insipid on their own. Ginger, spring onion, sesame and soy sauce can all be used to add flavour.

FRESH MUSHROOMS AND BAMBOO SHOOTS IN SHRIMP ROE SAUCE

Mushrooms have a fairly distinctive flavour in themselves, particularly if the dried kind are used, but the taste of this dish is made even stronger by the addition of shrimp roe.

溫公齋煲

VEGETARIAN CASSEROLE
Any number of vegetables
can be combined in this
casserole, including root
vegetables, leafy
vegetables, bean sprouts,
bamboo shoots or
aubergines. They are
cooked in meat stock or
orange stock, and mung
bean noodles or
transparent noodles, and
perhaps bean curd, may
be added. The resulting
semi-soup is a light
accompaniment to
heavier dishes.

蝦
子
嫩
笋
鮮
菇

Heat the oil in a pan. Add the bamboo shoots and fry for 1 minute, then add the mushrooms and fry for 1 minute. Remove, drain and set aside.

Heat 3-4 tbsp oil in a pan and add the ginger and garlic. When they have browned, remove them with a perforated spoon and discard.

Add the dried shrimp roes (or 2$\frac{1}{2}$ tsp shrimp sauce) and return the bamboo shoots and mushrooms to the pan. Add 1 tsp salt and 1 tsp sugar, stirring quickly, and cook for 1 minute.

Add the sauce ingredients, stirring continually over a high heat until the liquid is reduced to half. Serve hot.

VEGETARIAN CASSEROLE

250g (9oz) aubergine	2 tbsp red fermented bean curd
100g (4oz) French beans	450ml (16floz/2 cups) chicken
250g (9oz) Chinese cabbage	stock or water
6 medium black mushrooms	2 pieces fried bean curd
50g (2oz) mung bean noodles	1 tsp salt
225ml (8floz/1 cup) peanut oil	1$\frac{1}{2}$ tbsp cornflour blended with 1$\frac{1}{2}$
4 pieces sweet dried bean curd	tbsp water
4 slices ginger	1 tsp Chinese yellow wine
1 tsp chopped garlic	1 tsp sesame oil

Cut the aubergine into long, thick strips, the French beans in half and the cabbage lengthways into quarters.

Soak the black mushrooms in hot water for 30 minutes. Remove and discard the stems and cut the caps in half.

Soak the mung bean noodles in hot water for 10 minutes.

Heat the oil in a pan and fry all the vegetables for 1 minute over a high heat. Remove, drain and set aside.

Sauté the sweet dried bean curd over a low heat until slightly browned. Remove and set aside.

Heat 2 tbsp oil in a clay pot and add the ginger and garlic. Break the fermented red bean curd into pieces and add 2 tbsp to the pot, stirring over a high heat to release the aroma.

Place all the vegetables in the clay pot and cook, stirring continuously, for 2 minutes. Add the chicken stock or water, place the fried bean curd and sweet dried bean curd sheets on top of the vegetables and bring to the boil. Cover the pot, lower the heat and simmer for 10 minutes.

Add the mung bean noodles and salt, re-cover the pot and cook for another 2 minutes over high heat. Stir in the softened cornflour, add the Chinese yellow wine and sesame oil and serve.

Any kind of vegetables may be used in this recipe, but if you choose a delicate vegetable, such as lettuce, add it at the last minute. This is an excellent accompaniment for rice.

COLOURFUL BEAN SPROUTS

3 pieces dried, spiced bean curd
2 bell peppers
2 fresh red chilli peppers
40g (1½oz) salted sour cabbage
50g (2oz) leeks
1 tsp sugar
4 tbsp peanut oil
1½ tsp chopped garlic
1½ tsp chopped ginger
150g (5oz) bean sprouts

Seasonings
2 tsp oyster sauce
1 tsp monosodium glutamate
   (optional)
2 tsp soy sauce
½ tsp salt
1 tsp sugar
¼ tsp pepper
1 tbsp cornflour
4 tbsp stock
few drops of sesame oil

2 tsp rice wine

Cut the bean curd, bell peppers, chillies and salted sour cabbage into matchstick-size shreds, and cut the leeks slantwise into 5cm (2in) slices. Mix the cabbage with 1 tsp sugar.

Heat the pan until it is very hot and pour 1 tsp peanut oil into it. Add ½ tsp garlic and ½ tsp ginger. Stir-fry the bean sprouts for 30 seconds and put them on one side.

Reheat the pan until it is very hot and pour in 3 tbsp peanut oil. Add 1 tsp garlic and 1 tsp ginger and sauté until fragrant. Add the shredded bean curd, chillies and bell peppers and stir-fry over a high heat for 30 seconds. Add the bean sprouts and leeks. Stir-fry for another 30 seconds. Add the seasonings and continue to stir-fry for 10 seconds. Sprinkle with rice wine and serve.

FRIED MILK DAI LIANG COUNTY STYLE

450ml (16floz/2 cups) oil (for
   frying noodles and olive
   kernels)
50g (2oz) olive kernels
25g (1oz) rice-flour noodles
285ml (10floz/1¼ cups) fresh milk
170ml (6floz/¾ cup) unsweetened
   evaporated milk
7 egg whites

1 tbsp cornflour
½ tsp salt
3 tbsp oil
70g (2½oz) crab meat

Garnish
2 tsp chopped ham
2 tsp chopped coriander

Pour 450ml (16floz/2 cups) oil into a pan. When the oil is hot, fry the olive kernels for 5 seconds over medium heat. Remove the kernels and immediately add the dry rice noodles. As soon as they froth up and float, remove the noodles, drain away the oil on absorbent paper and put them on a serving dish to keep warm.

In a bowl mix together the fresh milk, evaporated milk, egg whites, cornflour and salt. Heat the pan until it is very hot and add

珊
瑚
荳
腐

CRISPY COATED CORAL BEAN
CURD
The bean curd is deep
fried briefly so that it is
firm enough to pick up
with chopsticks and is
dipped into the sauce.

SWEET BIRD'S NEST AND
GINSENG SOUP
The contrast in this dish
lies in the cost of the
ingredients. Ginseng of
the best quality can be
very expensive, and the
finest bird's nest actually
costs more than its
weight in gold. The sweet
soup, however, costs next
to nothing, being
basically rock sugar syrup
thickened with cornflour.

鴛鴦飯

YIN AND YANG RICE
Two colours of rice — the one plain white, the other coloured with tomato puree — are used in this dish to form the Taoist symbol, in which the opposites yin and yang form a complementary whole.

FRIED MILK DAI LIANG COUNTY STYLE
It is actually the skin of the milk that is fried. Milk thickened with cornflour is cooked until the skin is thick. The skin can then be skimmed off and fried on its own or used as a rich batter to coat meat or poultry.

107

大良炒鮮奶

3 tbsp oil. Then add the crab meat, olive kernels and milk mixture. Scrape the materials from the bottom and sides of the pan towards the centre until the ingredients are set. Remove from the pan and spread over the noodles. Garnish and serve.

SWEET BIRD'S NEST AND GINSENG SOUP

40g (1¹/₂oz) bird's nest
1 fresh ginseng root

900ml (32fl oz/4 cups) boiling
water
4 tbsp sugar

Soak the bird's nest in hot water for 4-5 hours.

Clean the ginseng root, cut it into thin slices and place the slices and boiling water in a china or porcelain container with a lid. Steam for 1 hour. You may prefer to use the ginseng root whole; if so, steam it for 2 hours.

Add the sugar, stirring to dissolve, and then the bird's nest. Steam for 5 minutes and serve.

YIN AND YANG RICE

Marinade
1 egg white
1 tbsp cornflour
1 tsp sesame oil
1 tsp salt

225g (8oz) chicken breast
250g (9oz) shrimps, shelled and
*   deveined*
4 tbsp peanut oil
1 tbsp shredded ginger
2 eggs, beaten
225g (8oz) cold plain cooked rice
2 tbsp light soy sauce
225ml (8fl oz/1 cup) chicken stock
225ml (8fl oz/1 cup) peanut oil
50g (2oz) peas

1 tsp salt
1 tsp chopped ginger
1 tsp chopped garlic

White sauce
8 tbsp chicken stock
2 tbsp milk
1 tbsp cornflour
1 tsp salt

Red sauce
1¹/₂ tbsp tomato ketchup
8 tbsp chicken stock
1 tbsp cornflour
1 tsp sugar
1 tbsp light soy sauce

Mix together the marinade ingredients in a bowl. Shred the chicken breasts and add to half of the marinade. Set aside.

Clean the shrimps and pat them dry. Mix them with the other half of the marinade in a bowl and refrigerate for 30 minutes.

Heat 4 tbsp oil in a pan and add 1 tbsp shredded ginger. When hot, add the beaten eggs, and when the eggs are partially set, add the rice. Stir-fry for 2 minutes, breaking up the egg with a spatula. Add the soy sauce and chicken stock and keep on stir-frying for 3 minutes. Transfer to a large dish.

Heat 225ml (8fl oz/1 cup) oil in a pan. Add the shrimps, stirring to separate. Remove and set aside. Add the chicken to the oil, again stirring to separate. Remove and set aside. Cook the peas in 8 tbsp water with 1 tsp salt for 5 minutes. Drain and set aside.

Heat 1 tbsp oil in the pan and add ½ tsp ginger and ½ tsp garlic. When the aroma rises, return the shrimps and peas to the pan. Add the white sauce ingredients and bring to the boil. Pour over one half of the dish of fried rice, using an S-shaped piece of foil to keep the sauce to one side of the dish.

Heat 1 tbsp oil in the pan and add ½ tsp ginger and ½ tsp garlic and when the aroma arises, return the chicken to the pan. Add the red sauce ingredients and bring to the boil. Pour over the fried rice on the other side of the foil. Remove the foil and serve.

CRISPY COATED CORAL BEAN CURD

400g (14oz) fresh shrimps
40g (1½oz) pork fat
1 tsp salt
½ tsp pepper
1 tsp sesame oil
2 egg whites
2 tsp cornflour
200g (7oz) bean curd, crushed

Pancakes
2 egg whites

20g (¾oz) cornflour

½l (20fl oz/3 cups) peanut oil

Sweet-and-sour sauce
4 tsp vinegar
3½ tsp sugar
2 tsp tomato ketchup
1 tsp Worcestershire sauce
2 tsp minced red chilli
salt to taste

Shell and devein shrimps. Wash them in salt water, drain and pat them dry with a paper towel. Crush the shrimps with the flat side of chopper.

Dice the pork fat into small cubes and put the shrimps, pork fat, salt, pepper, sesame oil, 2 egg whites and the cornflour into a bowl. Stir the ingredients in one direction until they are sticky, then add the crushed bean curd and continue to stir until well mixed.

To make the pancakes beat the egg whites and add the cornflour, stirring and mixing thoroughly. Heat a frying pan, rub it with peanut oil and add sufficient egg white and cornflour mixture to make a wafer-thin pancake. Peel and set aside. Continue until all the pancake mixture is used.

Flatten 1 tsp of the shrimp mixture on the palm of your hand and coat it with a little dry cornflour. Wrap the mixture in one of the pancakes to form a roll about 4 × 8cm (1½ × 3in).

Heat the peanut oil and deep fry the rolls at a moderate heat until they are brown.

Serve with sweet-and-sour sauce with minced chilli.

CHICKEN IN A NEST

1kg (2lb) chicken	*1 tbsp Chinese yellow wine*
	2 tbsp cornflour
Marinade	
1 tbsp oyster sauce	*4-6 medium black mushrooms*
1 tbsp light soy sauce	*250g (9oz) bamboo shoots*
1 tsp dark soy sauce	*100g (4oz) self-raising flour*
1 tsp sesame oil	*8 tbsp water*
1 tsp sugar	*1 tbsp sugar*
1 tsp salt	

Cut the chicken into bite-size pieces. Mix together the ingredients for the marinade, add the chicken pieces and set aside.

Soak the black mushrooms in hot water for 30 minutes. Cut off and discard the stems and cut each cap into eight pieces.

Cut the bamboo shoots into slices approximately the same size as the mushroom pieces. Add the black mushrooms and bamboo shoots to the chicken, mix well and set aside.

Put the flour in a mixing bowl, add the water and sugar and mix well. Knead the dough on a lightly floured surface until it is smooth, then leave it to stand for 30 minutes.

Roll the dough into a 'sausage' and divide it into small balls, approximately 25mm (1in) in diameter. Flatten the ball slightly with the palm of your hand and work it into a bowl shape, about 5cm (2in) in diameter. Place the bowl on a piece of paper about 5cm (2in) square and in each bowl or nest put about 2 tbsp of the chicken, black mushroom and bamboo shoot mixture.

Steam the nests for 10 to 15 minutes. Serve.

PORK DUMPLINGS

DIMSUM (*see opposite*) Rice in lotus leaves surrounded by *dimsum*. 1 Cock's-comb dumplings, 2 Pork liver and shrimp, 3 Pork dumplings, 4 Chicken in a nest, 5 Rice in lotus leaves, 6 Beef and black mushrooms, 7 Shrimp dumplings, 8 Chicken bundles, 9 Squid stuffed with shrimps.

Wrapper	**Marinade**
100g (4oz) plain flour	*1 tbsp light soy sauce*
2 eggs	*½ tsp sugar*
¼ tsp baking soda	*½ tsp sesame oil*
	½ tsp pepper
Filling	*1 tsp Chinese yellow*
3 medium black mushrooms	*wine*
500g (1¼lb) fillet of pork	*1 tbsp cornflour*
100g (4oz) pork fat	*1 egg white*
	1 tsp salt

Make the wrappers for the dumplings by putting the flour in a mixing bowl. Make a well in the centre, add the eggs and baking soda and mix well. Knead the dough on a lightly floured surface until it is smooth.

Roll it into a 'sausage', approximately 3cm (1½in) in diameter,

cover it with a towel and leave to stand for 20 minutes.

Pull the dough apart and roll the pieces between your palms into small balls approximately 3cm (1in) in diameter. Flatten each ball slightly, dust with flour and roll out into a thin pancake.

Soak the black mushroom in hot water for 30 minutes. Cut off and discard the stems and finely dice the caps.

Cut the fillet of pork and the pork fat into small cubes and mix the pork and mushroom pieces with the marinade ingredients, stirring with a fork until the mixture becomes sticky.

Place one wrapper in the palm of your hand. Put 1 tsp (heaped) of the filling in the centre of the wrapper and squeeze the edges gently together until it looks something like a purse, but leave the top open. If you wish, trim away any excess wrapper, but this is not essential. Continue until all the wrappers are used. Steam over a high heat for 10 to 15 minutes. Serve.

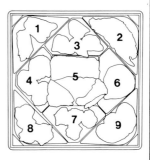

RICE IN LOTUS LEAVES

600g (1½lb) long grain rice	80g (3½oz) crab meat
150g (5oz) dried scallops (if dried scallops are too expensive, use dried shrimps)	2 tbsp chopped ham
	1 tsp sesame oil
	¼tsp pepper
2l (80floz/10 cups) water	1 tbsp soy sauce
150g (5oz) roast duck	1 tsp salt
100g (4oz) fresh shrimps	1 large dried lotus leaf

Wash and drain the rice. Put the scallops into the water and boil them over a low heat until only about half the water is left.

Put the rice in a large bowl or basin together with the scallop soup and steam the mixture for 15-20 minutes.

Mix the steamed rice and scallops with all the other ingredients and wrap the rice mixture in a large lotus leaf, which has been cleaned by rinsing under boiling water and steamed for another 30 minutes. Secure the lotus-leaf-wrapped parcel with string and place it in a steamer to steam for another 10 minutes.

Serve by bringing the 'parcel' to the table, to be unwrapped on serving.

STEAMED PORK LIVER AND SPARE RIB OF PORK

250g (9oz) pork liver	1 tsp Chinese yellow wine
500g (1¼lb) spare rib of pork	1 tsp sugar
	1 tbsp cornflour
Marinade	
1 tbsp light soy sauce	1 tbsp ground bean paste
1 tsp dark soy sauce	1 tbsp chopped shallot
1 tsp sesame oil	

Cut the pork liver into slices (3mm/⅛in), soak the pieces in water and set aside. Chop the spare rib of pork into bite-size pieces (3 × 4cm/1½ × 1¾in).

Blend together the ingredients for the marinade and add three-quarters of the mixture to the spare rib and the remaining quarter to the liver.

Add the bean paste and chopped shallot to the spare rib and mix well.

Lay the spare rib in the bottom of small dishes — do not pile it up — and place two or three pieces of liver on top.

Bring 3l (6 pints) water to the boil in a large wok with a bamboo steamer in it. Put the small dishes of spare rib and liver in the steamer, cover and steam over a high heat for 12-15 minutes. Serve.

SQUID STUFFED WITH SHRIMPS

100g (4oz) dried squid	2 tbsp cornflour
100g (4oz) pork fat	½ tsp pepper
400g (14oz) shrimps, shelled and	¼ tsp salt
deveined	1 egg white

Soak the dried squid in hot water for 1 hour before cutting it into pieces 3 × 6cm (1½ × 2½in).

Cut the pork fat into 3mm (⅛in) cubes and blanch in boiling water for 2 minutes. Remove and drain.

Pound the shrimps with the flat side of a cleaver and place them in a mixing bowl. Add 1 tbsp cornflour, the salt and pepper and the egg white to the shrimps and, using a fork, stir in one direction only until the mixture becomes sticky. Add the pork fat and stir until sticky again. Set aside.

Take a piece of squid and dust one side with some of the remaining cornflour. Place 1 tbsp of the shrimp and pork fat mixture on the floured side of the squid and press gently. Continue until all the squid pieces and shrimp mixture are used.

Arrange the stuffed squid on a plate and steam for 10 minutes over a high heat.

BEEF AND BLACK MUSHROOMS

100g (4oz) pork fat	2½ tsp salt
500g (1¼lb) minced beef	12 small black mushrooms
8 tbsp stock	1 tsp sugar
1 tbsp cornflour	1 tbsp peanut oil
1 tsp sesame oil	

Cut the pork fat into tiny cubes (3mm/⅛in) and blanch the pieces in boiling water for 1 minute. Rinse under the tap.

Put the minced beef, pork fat, stock, cornflour, sesame oil and 1½ tsp salt in a mixing bowl and stir, in one direction only, with a fork until the mixture becomes sticky.

Soak the black mushrooms in hot water for 30 minutes, remove and discard the stems and place the caps in a bowl. Add 1 tsp salt, the sugar and peanut oil and mix well. Steam the mushrooms over a medium heat for 5 minutes and set aside.

Divide the beef into 12 portions, moulding each portion into an egg shape, and place one mushroom on top of each 'egg'.

Use six small dishes and place two of the beef and mushroom 'eggs' in each dish. Steam over a high heat for 5 minutes and serve.

點心

A WIDE RANGE of *dimsum* is shown here in the bamboo baskets in which they are steamed.
(*Top row, from left to right*) Squid stuffed with shrimps; Steamed pork liver and spare rib of pork; Chicken in a nest; (*centre*) Pork Dumplings; Chicken bundles; (*bottom row*) Shrimp dumplings; Cock's-comb dumplings; Beef and black mushrooms.

CHICKEN BUNDLES

300g (11oz) supreme of chicken	*2 tsp cornflour*
(preferably with skin on)	*100g (4oz) roast fillet of pork*
2 tsp light soy sauce	*3 medium black mushrooms*
¹/₂ tsp sugar	*2 hard-boiled eggs*
¹/₄ tsp sesame oil	*200g (7oz) Chinese cabbage*
¹/₈ tsp pepper	

Cut the supreme of chicken into 5 × 3cm (2 × 1¹/₂in) pieces and mix the pieces with the soy sauce, sugar, sesame oil, pepper and cornflour. Set aside.

Cut the roast fillet of pork into 1cm (¹/₂in) slices and then into 5 × 1cm (2 × ¹/₂in) sticks. Set aside.

Soak the black mushrooms in hot water for 30 minutes. Remove and discard the stems and cut the caps into 5 × 1cm (2 × ¹/₂in) sticks. Set aside.

Cut each hard-boiled egg into eight pieces and set aside.

Blanch the cabbage in 450ml (16floz/2 cups) boiling salted water for 5 minutes, remove from the water, cut into 10 × 2cm (4 × ³/₄in) strips and set aside.

On each strip of cabbage place some chicken, roast pork and black mushroom pieces and, at the top, near to one end, a piece of egg. Roll the cabbage up to make a neat bundle. Continue with each strip of cabbage until all the ingredients are used.

Put two bundles into each small dish and steam over a high heat for 7-10 minutes. Serve.

SHRIMP DUMPLINGS

Wrapper	*100g (4oz) shredded bamboo*
see Pork Dumplings (page 110)	*shoot*
	1 tbsp lard
Filling	*1 tsp sesame oil*
600g (1¹/₂lb) shrimps, shelled and	*¹/₂ tsp pepper*
deveined	*1¹/₂ tsp sugar*
100g (4oz) cooked pork fat	*2 tsp salt*

Put all ingredients for the filling in a mixing bowl and stir until the mixture becomes sticky. Set aside.

Take one wrapper and place 1 tsp filling in the centre. Fold the wrapper up, working with both hands to seal the dumpling. Push the upper edge gently towards the left and make ruffles along the top of the dumpling. Steam the dumplings over a very high heat for 8-10 minutes and serve.

SPRING ROLLS

2 medium black mushrooms	4 tbsp peanut oil
100g (4oz) Chinese chives	1 tsp chopped ginger
250g (9oz) fillet of pork	1 tsp chopped garlic
	500g (1¼lb) bean sprouts
Marinade	1 tsp salt
2 tsp light soy sauce	20 spring roll wrappers
¼ tsp sesame oil	1 egg white
2 tsp cornflour	900ml (32floz/4 cups) peanut oil
1 tsp Chinese yellow wine	(to fry spring rolls)

Soak the black mushrooms in hot water for 30 minutes. Remove and discard the stems and cut the caps into fine shreds. Set aside.

Cut the Chinese chives into 4cm (1¾in) lengths. Set aside.

Finely shred the fillet of pork into pieces approximately 5cm (2in) long. Blend together the ingredients for the marinade and mix with the pork. Set aside.

Heat 2 tbsp oil in a pan and add ½ tsp ginger and ½ tsp garlic. Add the bean sprouts and mushrooms and stir-fry for 2 minutes.

Add the Chinese chives, stir-frying for 30 seconds, add 1 tsp salt, stir and remove from the heat. Set aside.

Heat 2 tbsp oil in the pan and add the remaining ginger and garlic. Add the pork, stir-frying for 1 minute over a medium heat, then increase the heat to very high. Return the bean sprouts, chives and mushrooms to the pan and stir-fry for 30 seconds over a very high heat. Remove, drain and set aside.

On each spring roll wrapper place approximately 3 tbsp bean sprouts and pork. Fold over the side of the wrapper nearest to you and then fold in the ends. Roll the wrapper into a cylinder, wetting the open side with egg white and pressing gently to secure. Repeat with the remaining ingredients to make 20 spring rolls.

Heat 900ml (32floz/4 cups) oil in the pan. Add the spring rolls and fry them over a low heat until they are nicely golden in colour, but do not use a high heat.

Serve the spring rolls hot. They may be eaten with Worcestershire sauce to enhance their flavour.

COCK'S-COMB DUMPLINGS

The wrappers are prepared in the same way as for Pork Dumplings (see page 110), but 2 tbsp chopped water chestnut and 1 tbsp chopped coriander are added to the filling. The dumplings are made and cooked as Pork Dumplings.

炸
蝦
丸

炸雪棗

SICHUAN CHICKEN

250g (9oz) fresh chicken fillet	40g (1½oz) lettuce
2 tsp shrimp sauce	1 tsp crushed peppercorns
½ tsp dark soy sauce	⅔ tbsp spring onion shavings
1 tsp monosodium glutamate (optional)	2 dried chilli peppers, finely chopped
1 tsp cornflour	3-4 drops sesame oil
450ml (16floz/2 cups) peanut oil	1 tsp rice wine

Slice the chicken fillet into pieces 5mm (¼in) thick and pound the meat to tenderize it. Mix the chicken with 1 tsp shrimp sauce, ½ tsp dark soy sauce, ½ tsp monosodium glutanate (if used) and 1 tsp cornflour.

Heat the pan until it is hot and pour 2 tbsp oil into it. Stir-fry the chicken over medium heat until it is almost done (about 1½ minutes). Remove the chicken from the pan to drain.

Stir-fry the lettuce in 4 tbsp very hot oil over high heat and remove immediately from the pan to drain away the oil. Arrange the lettuce around the edge of a plate.

Reheat the pan until very hot and pour in 1 tbsp oil. Stir-fry the crushed peppercorns with the spring onion shavings until fragrant, then add the chopped chilli followed by the chicken. Add 1 tsp shrimp sauce, ½ tsp monosodium glutamate (if used), the sesame oil and the rice wine. Stir and sauté for a short while over high heat. Remove and place in the centre of the plate surrounded by the quick-fried lettuce leaves.

DEEP-FRIED CRAB MEAT BALLS

2 pieces dried bean curd sheet	1 tbsp chopped leek (white part only)
225g (8oz) shrimps, shelled and deveined	1 tbsp chopped spring onion
50g (2oz) pork fat	1 tsp salt
70g (2½ oz) water chestnuts	½ tsp pepper
1 egg white	100g (4oz) crab meat
2 tbsp cornflour	¾l (20floz/3 cups) peanut oil

Soak the dried bean curd sheets in water until they have softened. Remove and pat dry. Set aside. Chop and mince the shrimps and dice the pork fat and water chestnuts into small pieces.

Place the minced shrimps, the egg white and cornflour in a mixing bowl and, using a fork, stir in one direction until the mixture becomes sticky and firm. Add the pork and continue stirring until the mixture is thick and firm.

COMBINATION STARTERS (*On previous page*) An unusual hot *hors d'oeuvre* from Chiu Chow, a coastal town renowned for its seafood and dipping sauces. Some of these starters are braised or stir-fried, others are coated in batter and deep-fried. They are all presented on the same plate.

炸
雪
棗

Add the water chestnuts, stirring and mixing well, and then the chopped leek, the chopped spring onion, the salt and pepper, and the crab meat, mixing each ingredient in thoroughly.

Place the bean curd sheet on a board. Put the shrimp and crab meat mixture on it, making it into the shape of a thick sausage about 25mm (1in) in diameter. Roll the bean curd sheet firmly around the mixture, trimming off any excess at the ends.

Place the 'sausage' on a heat-proof platter, and steam it over a high heat for 7 minutes. Remove, set aside and when it has cooled, cut it into 3cm (1½in) slices.

Heat the oil in a pan. When it is hot, add the crab meat slices. Reduce the heat to low and fry until the bean curd wrapper is nicely golden in colour. Serve with Chiu Chow tangerine jam.

Deep-fried prawn balls and crab balls are often served together, so it is advisable to double the quantity given in the prawn ball recipes and use half of the prawn mixture in conjunction with the crab meat dish.

SWEET-AND-SOUR PORK ROLLS

250g (9oz) fillet of pork
250g (9oz) pork fat
300g (11oz) water chestnuts
75g (3oz) spring onions

Seasonings
1½ tsp five-spice powder
2 tsp salt
2 tsp sugar

1 large piece pork fat

2 tbsp cornflour, blended with
    water
½l (20fl oz/3 cups) peanut oil
1 tbsp shredded ginger
8 tbsp sweet-and-sour sauce (see
    page 37)

Garnish
3 pineapple rings, each cut into
    four pieces

Shred the fillet of pork, pork fat, water chestnuts and spring onions and put them in a mixing bowl. Add the seasonings and mix thoroughly.

Flatten the large piece of pork fat on a lightly floured board. Place the shredded mixture on the fat and roll it up to make a sausage 25mm (1in) in diameter. Trim away any excess fat. Seal the ends with the blended cornflour and cut the 'sausage' into 3cm (1½in) sections. Set aside.

Heat the oil in a pan and add the sliced pork rolls. Fry over a high heat for 1 minute, reduce the heat to low and simmer for 4 minutes. Remove and set aside.

Heat 2 tbsp oil in the pan, add the ginger, then add the sweet-and-sour sauce and bring to the boil. Return the sliced pork rolls to the pan and sauté for 30 seconds, ensuring that every piece is coated with sauce. Garnish with the pineapple pieces and serve.

煎
蠔
蛋

OYSTER OMELETTE
Seafood omelettes are
typical of Chinese coastal
cooking. This Chiu Chow
version uses the strong
flavour of oysters, which
combines well with egg,
which in this case is
stir-fried.

STEAMED LOBSTER
Steaming lobster
produces a purer taste
than frying, and if ginger
and spring onion are
used, the flavour is more
delicate than with other
methods of cooking.

梅子鯉魚煲

SPARE RIB OF PORK, CARP AND
SALTED PLUM IN A CLAY POT
This is an unusual but
happy combination, the
acidity of the pickled
plum tempering the
richness of the carp and
pork. The surface fat
should be skimmed off
before serving, to leave a
highly flavoured clear
broth.

STEAMED EEL WITH PICKLED
PLUM AND SOY BEAN PASTE
Eel, being rich, goes well
with pickled plum. The
addition of bean paste, a
northern speciality, is
unexpected in a dish
from Chiu Chow, which is
just 200 miles from Hong
Kong.

123

FRIED PRAWN BALLS

225g (8oz) fresh prawns, shelled	1 tsp salt
80g (3½oz) water chestnuts	½ tsp monosodium glutamate
50g (2oz) lean and fat pork (20	(optional)
per cent fat)	½ tsp of pepper

Seasonings
1½ tbsp chopped white of leek · 50g (2oz) flour
1½ tbsp chopped spring onion · 450ml (16floz/2 cups) peanut oil
1 egg (to fry the prawn balls)

Chop and mince the prawns and dice the water chestnuts and pork into coarse grains.

Put the prawns into a bowl and stir until the mixture is sticky. Add the water chestnuts, pork and seasonings and mix well. Add the flour.

Heat the oil in a pan until it is smoking hot. Roll the prawn mixture into small balls about 2cm (¾in) in diameter and fry them until they start to turn brown. The mixture makes more than 20 prawn balls. Serve with Chiu Chow tangerine jam as a dip.

STEAMED EEL WITH PICKLED PLUM AND SOY BEAN PASTE

1kg (2lb) freshwater eel	2 tsp dark soy sauce
2 tbsp salt	2 tsp chopped garlic
4-6 pickled plums (remove and	1-2 tsp red chilli, finely shredded
discard the stones)	2 tbsp peanut oil
1 tbsp sugar	1 tbsp chopped coriander
2 tbsp soy bean paste	

Rub the eel with 2 tbsp salt. Put it in a basin and pour over it approximately 900ml (32floz/4 cups) boiling water. Clean and pat dry. Cut off the back fin, slit it open from the back and remove the bones.

Cut the eel into sections 5cm (2in) long and place them on large plate.

Mix together the pickled plums, sugar, soy bean paste, dark soy sauce, chopped garlic and finely shredded red chilli and spread evenly over the eel. Steam over medium heat for 35 minutes. Pour 2 tbsp very hot (boiling) peanut oil over the fish, sprinkle with the chopped coriander and serve.

The pickled plum brings a special lightness to what might otherwise be a rather heavy dish, while the long steaming time makes the eel melt in the mouth.

煎
蠔
蛋

OYSTER OMELETTE

4 medium oysters
1 tbsp cornflour
4 eggs
2 stems spring onion
1 stem coriander

$^1/_2$ tsp sesame oil
1 tsp pepper
1 tsp salt
2 tbsp peanut oil

Clean the oysters, cut them into small pieces (5mm/$^1/_4$in) and mix them with 1 tbsp cornflour. Set aside. Beat the eggs together lightly. Finely chop the spring onion and coriander and add to the egg.

Blanch the diced oyster in boiling water for 30 seconds. Drain and add the sesame oil, pepper and salt. Mix well.

Heat a pan over medium heat and add 2 tbsp peanut oil. Pour half the egg mixture into the pan and half of the diced oyster. When the edge of the omelette browns slightly turn it over to complete cooking. Repeat with the rest of the egg and diced oyster. Serve on well-heated dish.

SPARE RIB OF PORK, CARP AND SALTED PLUM IN A CLAY POT

500g (1$^1/_4$lb) spare rib of pork
1kg (2lb) carp or any other
   freshwater fish
$^1/_2$l (20fl oz/3 cups) chicken stock

$^1/_2$l (20fl oz/3 cups) water
3-4 salted plums
6 slices ginger
2 stalks spring onions

Chop the spare rib across the bones into bite-size pieces and blanch them in boiling water for 2 minutes. Remove and set aside.

Clean the carp thoroughly, paying particular attention to the inside of the cavity. Set aside.

Bring the chicken stock and water to the boil in a clay pot. Add all the ingredients and when the mixture boils again, lower the heat to medium. Cook for 5 minutes. Lower the heat further and simmer gently for 15 more minutes. Serve.

STEAMED LOBSTER

1kg (2lb) fresh or frozen lobster
   (cooked red lobster is not
   suitable)
6 slices ginger
50g (2oz) chicken fat, finely

   chopped
2 tbsp peanut oil
1 tbsp shrimp sauce
1 tsp Chinese yellow wine
1 tbsp light soy sauce

(Recipe continued on page 128)

鹹菜海鮮湯

PICKLED CABBAGE AND
CHICKEN CLEAR SOUP
Pickled cabbage, known
in China as 'snow pickle',
is used extensively along
the Yangtze River as well
as in Chiu Chow. It gives
the chicken a slightly
vinegary and salty flavour.

鹹菜海鮮湯

PURSE CHICKEN
Another Chiu Chow dish
eaten in other parts of
China. The purse is a
small omelette made with
a tablespoon or two of
beaten egg which is
shallow fried and
wrapped around a variety
of ingredients.

清
燕
龍
蝦

Chop the lobster flesh, including the shell, into large bite-size pieces and spread them out on a plate. (Do not pile the pieces in the centre of the plate.) Sprinkle the ginger and chopped chicken fat on top of the lobster pieces.

Bring 1 l (40 fl oz/5 cups) water to the boil in a wok. Place a rack in the wok and put the plate on top of the rack. Steam the lobster over a very high heat for 5-7 minutes. Remove, drain any liquid from the lobster into a bowl and set aside.

Heat 2 tbsp peanut oil in a pan. Add the liquid from the steamed lobster and the shrimp sauce, yellow wine and light soy sauce to make a sauce. Pour over the lobster and serve.

PURSE CHICKEN

250g (9oz) broccoli
2 medium black mushrooms
50g (2oz) bamboo shoots
50g (2oz) water chestnuts
1 tbsp salt
5 tbsp peanut oil
3 spring onions
150g (5oz) chicken breast, diced
2 tsp egg white
1/2 tsp cornflour
1 tbsp chopped coriander, stem and leaf

Pancakes
3 egg whites
2 tsp cornflour
3 tbsp chicken stock

strands of onion
2 tbsp crab roe

Sauce
170ml (6fl oz/3/4 cup) chicken stock
1 tsp sesame oil
2 tsp Chinese yellow wine
1 tsp salt

Cut the broccoli into shavings, wash in salted water and set aside.

Soak the black mushrooms in hot water for 30 minutes. Remove and discard the stems, finely chop the caps and set aside.

Finely chop the bamboo shoot and water chestnuts and set aside. Bring 225ml (8fl oz/1 cup) water to the boil, add 1 tbsp salt and 1 tbsp oil and cook the broccoli spears for 5 minutes. Blanch the spring onions for 30 seconds. Remove and set aside.

Dice the chicken finely and mix it with 2 tsp of egg white and 1/2 tsp of cornflour. Set aside.

Heat 2 tbsp oil in pan. Add the black mushrooms, water chestnut, bamboo shoots, coriander and the chicken mixture. Stir and cook for 1 1/2 minutes over a low heat. Remove, drain and set aside.

Mix together the pancake ingredients. Heat the pan and grease the bottom with oil. Spoon 1 tbsp of the pancake mixture into the centre of pan and make a thin pancake over low heat. Repeat this process until all mixture is used up. (The ingredients given will make approximately 20 pancakes.)

Take one pancake and spoon 1 tbsp of the chicken and vege-table filling into the centre, gather up the edges and tie the top of

鹹
菜
海
鮮
湯

the bundle with a strand of onion (use the green part only). Put ½ tsp crab roe on top in the centre of the bundle.

Arrange the purses in the centre of a plate, sprinkle with broccoli and steam over medium heat for 5 minutes.

Heat 2 tbsp oil in a pan and add the sauce ingredients. Bring the sauce to the boil, stir and pour over the purses before serving.

PICKLED CABBAGE AND CHICKEN CLEAR SOUP

250g (9oz) pickled cabbage	*½ tsp sesame oil*
250g (9oz) chicken breasts	*1 tsp cornflour*
Marinade	*900ml (32floz/4 cup) chicken*
1 egg white	*stock*
1 tbsp light soy sauce	*225ml (8floz/1 cup) water*
	4 slices ginger

Soak the pickled cabbage in 1l (40floz/5 cups) salted water for 2 hours. Rinse under the tap, squeezing several times. Cut into strips 2 × 7cm (¾ × 3in) long.

Cut the chicken breast meat into thin slices (25 × 50 × 5mm/1 × 2 × ¼in). Mix the marinade, add the chicken and set aside.

Put the chicken stock, water, ginger and cabbage in a pot and bring to the boil. Reduce the heat and simmer for 15 minutes.

Bring 450ml (16floz/2 cups) water to the boil. Add the chicken slices, stir to separate and remove immediately. Drain the chicken and transfer the pieces to the soup in the pot. Simmer for 3 minutes and serve.

You may prefer to use prawns or shrimps, squid and fillet of fish instead of the chicken and make a seafood soup.

DUCKLING AND SALTED LIME CLEAR SOUP

2kg (4lb) duckling	*1 salted lime*
900ml (32floz/4 cups) chicken	*4 slices ginger*
stock	

Clean the duck, taking care to remove and discard any excess fat in the cavity and to remove the 'parson's nose'.

Boil 2l (4 pints/10 cups) water and blanch the duck for 5 minutes. Remove and set aside.

Put 900ml (32floz/4 cups) water and the chicken stock into a casserole with a lid. Add the duck, cutting it up if necessary, the salted lime and ginger. Cook covered over a low heat for 3-4 hours. Serve.

芥
蘭
牛
丸

STIR-FRIED BEEF BALLS WITH
DRIED FISH AND CHINESE KALE
Because the meat is
minced, the beef balls
need cooking only briefly.
This recipe calls for
Chinese kale, but spinach
would do equally well.
Sometimes water
chestnuts are used for
crunchiness and the dish
may be flavoured with
soy bean paste, sugar and
ginger.

STIR-FRIED MINCED PORK,
CHILLI, MUSHROOMS AND
BLACK OLIVES
This very unusual
combination of olives and
chilli could only occur in
Chiu Chow, which
borders on olive-growing
regions (olives are very
rare in Chinese cooking)
and is also influenced by
the hotness of Sichuan
and Hunan cooking.

雞火砂鍋

STEWED HAM AND MUSTARD GREEN IN A CLAY POT
Another Chiu Chow dish seldom eaten in other parts of China. The mustard greens are slightly vinegary and salty, which counteracts the richness of the ham. But care must be taken during long cooking that the dish does not become too salty.

DUCKLING AND SALTED LIME CLEAR SOUP
The purpose of the salted lime is to counteract the richness of the duckling. A good deal of fat needs to be skimmed off the liquid before serving, but the flavour is interesting.

榨
菜
肉
碎

STIR-FRIED MINCED PORK, CHILLI, MUSHROOMS AND BLACK OLIVES

Marinade
1 tsp cornflour
2 tsp light soy sauce
1 tsp sugar
1 tsp Chinese yellow wine
2 tbsp peanut oil

250g (9oz) minced pork

100g (4oz) button mushrooms
1 red chilli
1 tbsp black olives in sesame oil
   (black olives for cocktails could
   be a good substitute)
1 tbsp peanut oil
1 tsp chopped garlic

Prepare the marinade and marinate the minced pork. Set aside.

Slice the button mushrooms and finely shred the red chilli. Chop the black olives into small pieces.

Heat 1 tbsp oil in pan. Add the garlic and when the aroma arises, add the minced pork. Stir and cook over medium heat for 3 minutes.

Add the black olives, button mushrooms and red chilli and stir-fry over medium heat for 2 minutes. This is a wonderful dish to accompany plain cooked rice, rice soup or boiled noodles.

STIR-FRIED BEEF BALLS WITH DRIED FISH AND CHINESE KALE

500g (1¼lb) frozen beef balls
225-250g (8-12oz) dried fish
   (sole)
500g (1¼lb) Chinese kale
8 tbsp peanut oil
1 tsp chopped ginger

4 tbsp chicken stock
1 tbsp fish or shrimp sauce
1 tsp sugar
1 tsp chopped garlic
2 tsp Chinese yellow wine

Defrost the beef balls and rinse them under the tap. Cut about a quarter of the way through each beef ball and set aside.

Remove and discard the bone of the dried fish and break the meat into bite-size pieces. Fry the fish pieces in 8 tbsp oil until nicely browned. Remove, drain and set aside.

Cut the Chinese kale into lengths 4 × 5cm (1¾ × 2in).

Heat 3 tbsp oil in a pan. Add the ginger and Chinese kale, stir-frying over a very high heat for 1 minute. Add 4 tbsp chicken stock, cover and cook over a very high heat for a further minute.

Uncover the pan and add 1 tbsp fish or shrimp sauce and 1 tsp sugar. Stir rapidly over very high heat for 1 minute.

Add 2 tbsp of oil, the garlic, beef balls and Chinese yellow wine, stir-frying for 2 minutes. Return the fried dried sole to the pan, stir for 30 seconds and serve.

400g (1lb) minced beef	*1½ tbsp cornflour*
1 egg white	*½ tbsp sesame oil*
4-5 tbsp water	*½ tsp pepper*
1½ tbsp salt	

If frozen beef balls are not available, you can make your own. Put all the ingredients in a mixing bowl and use a fork to stir — in one direction only — until the mixture becomes sticky and firm. Make up to 20 small meat balls, about 2cm (¾in) in diameter.

Bring about 900ml (32fl oz/4 cups) water to the boil, add the beef balls and remove them when they float to the top. Set aside and follow the recipe above.

YIN AND YANG VEGETABLE SOUP

500g (1¼lb) spinach leaves	*4 tbsp peanut oil*
1 tsp baking soda	*2 tsp Chinese yellow wine*
250g (9oz) button mushrooms	*900ml (32fl oz/4 cups) chicken*
100g (4oz) chicken breast meat	*stock*
1 egg white	*6 tbsp cornflour*
2 tsp salt	

Blanch the spinach for 2 minutes in 450ml (16fl oz/2 cups) boiling water with 1 tsp baking soda added. Remove and rinse under the tap for 1 minute. Drain the leaves before chopping them finely. Set aside. Chop the mushrooms finely. Set aside. Finely mince the chicken breast and mix with the egg white and 1 tsp salt. Set aside.

Heat 2 tbsp oil in a pan. Sauté the minced spinach for 3 minutes, add 1 tsp of Chinese yellow wine and 1 tsp of salt and stir together. Add 450ml (16fl oz/2 cups) chicken stock to the pan having first mixed 3 tbsp of the stock with 3 tbsp cornflour. Bring the stock to the boil and slowly stir in the cornflour.

Place an S-shaped piece of greased cardboard in the centre of a soup tureen to divide the bowl into two. Pour the spinach soup into one side of the bowl, holding the cardboard upright by placing a glass of water against it on the empty side.

Heat 2 tbsp oil. Add the mushrooms, sauté for 1 minute and add 1 tsp of Chinese yellow wine. Take 3 tbsp of the remaining stock and mix with 3 tbsp cornflour. Add the rest of the chicken stock to the pan, bring to the boil and slowly stir in the blended cornflour. When it boils, stir in the minced chicken and mix well.

Pour the chicken soup into the other half of the soup tureen, first removing the glass of water. Take out the cardboard as gently as possible. The one bowl of soup is then presented and served in the two colours of Yin and Yang.

YIN AND YANG VEGETABLE SOUP

太極大河素

YIN AND YANG VEGETABLE SOUP

As with yin and yang rice, different colours are used to form the Chinese symbol of unity in which positive and negative complement each other. The green part is usually made from a green vegetable. The white part is also usually vegetable, perhaps with milk or chicken added.

SHREDDED PORK, BLACK MUSHROOMS, CELERY AND NOODLES IN SESAME SAUCE
The combination of pork, black mushrooms and celery is common enough in China, but what makes this Chiu Chow dish unusual is the addition of a sesame sauce.

AROMATIC CHIU CHOW RICH
FISH SOUP
The Chinese seldom use
rice for soup. But this is a
thick soup, the
consistency of thin
porridge, which is eaten
for supper or perhaps for
breakfast rather than as
an accompaniment to
other dishes.

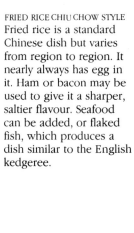

FRIED RICE CHIU CHOW STYLE
Fried rice is a standard
Chinese dish but varies
from region to region. It
nearly always has egg in
it. Ham or bacon may be
used to give it a sharper,
saltier flavour. Seafood
can be added, or flaked
fish, which produces a
dish similar to the English
kedgeree.

芥蘭炒飯

STEWED HAM AND MUSTARD GREEN IN A CLAY POT

225g (8oz) mustard green	**Sauce**
225g (8oz) cabbage	*1 tbsp oyster sauce*
6 medium black mushrooms	*1 tbsp light soy sauce*
50g (2oz) Chinese ham	*1 tsp dark soy sauce*
225ml (8floz/1 cup) peanut oil	*1 tsp sugar*
4 slices ginger	*1 tsp sesame oil*
225ml (8floz/1 cup) chicken stock	*2 tsp Chinese yellow wine*

Cut the mustard green into pieces 25 × 50mm (1 × 2in) and cut the cabbage into strips the same size.

Soak the mushrooms in hot water for 30 minutes. Remove and discard the stems and cut each cap into half.

Cut the ham into slices 20 × 40 × 2mm ($\frac{3}{4}$ × $1\frac{3}{4}$ × $\frac{1}{8}$in).

Heat the oil and fry the cabbage for 1 minute. Drain well and set aside. Fry the mustard green for 1 minute. Drain and set aside.

Heat 2 tbsp oil in a clay pot or casserole and add the mushrooms, cabbage and mustard green. Place the ham on top but do not mix. Add the chicken stock and bring to the boil, reduce the heat and simmer for 30-45 minutes. Add the sauce ingredients and simmer for 2 minutes. Serve in the clay pot or casserole.

SHREDDED PORK, BLACK MUSHROOMS, CELERY AND NOODLES IN SESAME SAUCE

50g (2oz) pork	**Sauce**
1 medium black mushroom	*2 tbsp sesame paste*
1 Chinese celery	*1 tbsp fish sauce or shrimp sauce*
4 packets dried egg noodles	*1 tsp sugar*
2 tbsp peanut oil	*1 tsp Chinese yellow wine*
	2 tbsp cornflour
	225ml (8floz/1 cup) chicken stock

Cut the pork into matchstick-size shreds. Soak the black mushroom in hot water for 30 minutes. Remove and discard the stem and chop the cap finely. Set aside. Chop the Chinese celery into small pieces.

Bring 2l (40floz/10 cups) water to the boil. Add the noodles, stirring to separate, and cook for 3 minutes. Transfer the noodles to a large pan of cold water. Return the noodles to boiling water and cook for 1 minute. Drain and place in a large bowl or on a plate. Set aside.

Heat 2 tbsp peanut oil in a pan. When hot, add the pork and stir-fry for 1 minute over high heat. Add the mushrooms and celery, and continue to cook for 30 seconds.

Add the sauce ingredients and bring to the boil. Return the noodles to the pan, stirring, and cook for another 30 seconds.

Transfer the noodles to a serving plate first and place the pork, mushroom and celery on top as a garnish. Pour the sauce over them and serve.

AROMATIC CHIU CHOW RICH FISH SOUP

150g (5oz) fillet of pomfret (sea bream) or other white fish	2-3 tbsp peanut oil
100g (4oz) squid	2 medium black mushrooms
1 tsp sesame oil	1 Chinese celery
1 tsp salt	1/2l (20floz/3 cups) chicken stock
1 fillet dried sole	225g (8oz) plain cooked rice

Cut the fillet of pomfret or whichever white fish you are using into thick slices and cut the squid into bite-size pieces. Mix the fish and squid with 1 tsp of sesame oil and 1 tsp of salt.

Break or chop the fillet of dried sole into tiny pieces and deep fry with 2-3 tbsp oil over low heat until crisp. Drain and set aside.

Soak the black mushrooms in hot water for 30 minutes. Remove and discard the stems and cut the caps into fine shreds. Chop the celery coarsely.

Bring the chicken stock to the boil and add the celery, black mushrooms and rice.

When the soup boils again, add the sliced fish and squid and when it boils again, sprinkle with chopped dried fish and serve.

FRIED RICE CHIU CHOW STYLE

100g (4oz) Chinese kale, stem only	2 eggs, lightly beaten
4 tbsp peanut oil	225g (8oz) cold plain cooked rice
2 tbsp shredded ginger	2 tbsp shrimp sauce
100g (4oz) shrimps, shelled and deveined	8 tbsp chicken stock

Dice the stems of the Chinese kale into small pieces.

Heat the oil in a pan and add the shredded ginger, shrimps and Chinese kale, stir-frying them for 1 minute.

Add the eggs (beaten for 10 seconds) and, when they are partly set, add the cold plain rice. Stir-fry over a very high heat. Scramble the eggs, breaking them into tiny pieces with your spoon or spatula.

Add the shrimp sauce and chicken stock and stir-fry over reduced heat for a further 3-5 minutes. Serve.

NORTHERN SCHOOL

BEAR'S PAW served on a gold dish for an Imperial banquet.

(*Opposite page*)
FRESHWATER AND SALTWATER shrimps on sale in a fish market.

Peking (or Beijing as it is now called) inevitably acquired a cosmopolitan cuisine as the city attracted cooks from other regions who introduced new dishes into the Peking school of cooking. Chefs came from as far south as Shandong and as far north as Manchuria, Mongolia and Sinkiang, and the presence of the Imperial court inevitably encouraged the development of a wonderful range of rich dishes. As the dynasties changed, the native Han Chinese cuisine was added to under the influence of Mongolian or Manchurian rulers, and now there are more than fifty different styles of cookery in what is known as the Peking school.

In general terms, northern Chinese food, from the Yellow River region around Peking, is more strongly flavoured than that of other schools, using a lot of bean paste, garlic and dark soy sauce. While other areas rely on rice as the staple food, northerners favour wheat and plump white dumplings, served steamed, boiled, baked or fried. Wheat noodles are the other main accompaniment or ingredient in a variety of dishes.

Inevitably, in the cool climate in which Peking shivers for six months of the year, 'hot' foods are paramount. Hot pots, the Mongolians' lasting influence, are also popular.

The original hot pot or 'fire kettle', is akin to those found in other northern lands, Korea, Japan and even Switzerland. Like the Mongolian self-service barbecueing griddles, the hot pot is a survivor of prehistoric times. Families or even the whole clan would gather around a massive charcoal-burning stove, as nomadic people everywhere still do. The westerner who has stood around a barbecue pit or camp-fire is part of the same tradition. Even when the Mongolians settled down, their tents becoming permanent homes, the need for warmth and their gregarious natures ensured the modified survival of the central cooking stove. The kitchen was the living room and the cooking range the table.

Meats were marinated, both to preserve them and to add flavours. Further taste was added with piquant sauces into which the griddled or boiled meat slices were dipped. Mutton was preferred to pork, for the nomadic, sheep-herding Mongolians loved their horses and ate their sheep.

Once they had been converted to the new religion, Muslim religious beliefs suited the Mongolians. There are still about four million Chinese Muslims, mostly living in the northern provinces, but all northerners enjoy mutton, unlike southern Chinese, who find the meat's smell unpleasantly heavy.

When the Mongolians conquered Peking their cooking styles came with them. They did not have far to travel as the present border of Inner Mongolia is only about 100 miles north of Peking. The Great Wall of China, the 2,200-year-old Chin dynasty line of defence, is just 40 miles north, although part of Peking's Hopei Province extends into the semi-autonomous People's Republic of Inner Mongolia (not to be confused with the Soviet Mongolian

People's Republic further north). Mongolian master-strategist Genghis Khan overcame the Great Wall, and the Mongol Yuan dynasty ruled the Chinese Empire from 1280 when Kublai Khan took the throne. There had been Tartar dynasties before (the Chin and Liao dynasties), but Kublai Khan's reign saw northern conquerors in their full might.

Apart from mutton, the Mongolians brought with them goats and the passion for game meat that was another culinary influence of a nomadic hunting people. In consequence, Chinese game feasts are looked on as northern-style meals and have an exotic appeal even for southern Chinese during their short winters.

Each animal has its special attributes, and through eating the animal, a diner feels he is absorbing those qualities. The consumption of game was another sign of Chinese beliefs in the curative values of food. As usual, sexual prowess was important and gained through deer horns or the penises of a wide variety of wild animals. Generally the game gave the strength and vigour with which northerners survived the rigours of winter.

At the Imperial court there was rarely need for frugality, and game feasts developed into gargantuan, marathon meals. During the rule of the Manchurians (the Ching dynasty) from 1644 to 1911, the Imperial banquet was a culinary orgy that rivalled anything a European renaissance court had prepared. The feasts started out fairly simply in the seventeenth century and were originally served to Emperors when they and their retinues visited southern cities. Less restricted by court protocol, the southern banquets were informal affairs that maintained the traditions of family gatherings. In Peking, however, where the women of the Imperial palaces were forbidden to dine with the men, the style changed.

THE PAVILION OF FLOATING GREEN in the Imperial Palace, Peking.

In their Man (Manchurian) and Han forms the Imperial banquets developed into three-day-long affairs. Bizarre and exotic dishes contrasted with the subtlest recipes collected during southern tours, for the Manchus, recognizing their superior cooking talents, imported cooks from the Yangtze River basin.

Being convinced numerologists, the Chinese insisted that an Imperial banquet should have 365 dishes, just as a famed herbalist had earlier identified 365 valued herbs. No wonder a banquet lasted three days even though the number of dishes was later reduced to 108! It should not be imagined that Imperial courtiers were gourmands rather than gourmets, however. Many of the dishes were prepared for display purposes only at breakfasts and lunches during the three days. The dinners were the main events, offering such exotica as elephant trunks, bear's paws, gorilla lips, camel humps and monkey brains, in an age when wildlife conservation was unheard of.

Today the most popular of the elaborate Imperial dishes is the Peking Duck. Glazed and roasted, the duck should be a specially-reared bird that has been force-fed as generously as a Strasbourg goose. The special pancakes served with the delicately-carved duck skin are one example of the fine flour products of the northern Chinese. Wheat, barley and other grains grew in the Yellow River plains. Rice did not — the climate was too harsh. Bean derivatives were another staple, as were green vegetables, most frequently varieties of Chinese cabbage, such as the one that honours Peking's nearby city of Tientsin.

Even with a majestic dish like Peking Duck, whose original recipe had 15,000 words, the Chinese abhorrence of waste was apparent. When the duck skin slivers were laid in their little pancakes, the sauce was not the plum variety used everywhere nowadays but a special fermented dough paste made from previous meals' leftover pancakes!

The other famed dish, Beggar's Chicken, which is not of Peking origin, but so popular in Peking restaurants overseas, could have a full book written about it. There are many legends regarding the origin of the clay-baked bird wrapped in a lotus leaf. One illustrates Chinese resourcefulness: it tells how a beggar who had no stove dug a hole in the ground and baked the wrapped chicken over hot ashes. A second legend records that the beggar needed to cook the bird in secret. Both legends admit that the beggar first stole the chicken. Chinese mythologists adore tales in which the rich or powerful are tricked by supposedly simple men! But Beggar's Chicken is certainly not simple. When the clay casing is smashed open and the cooked bird's flavours and aromas waft forth in a cloud of culinary incense, the anonymous beggar deserves to have achieved immortality as a culinary king.

A PEKING vegetable market.

As foreigners and Chinese restaurateurs have discovered, Peking food has various semi-theatrical facets. Noodle-making is one of them. It would be a waste for pasta-masters to hide their skills in a kitchen. In Hong Kong and in some leading Chinese restaurants overseas they are star turns at banquets, as culinary acrobatic jugglers swing and twist one length of dough into incredibly fine strands.

Noodles, pancakes, 'silk thread' bread and heavy *dimsum* pastries filled up a northerner but would not protect an ordinary eater against winter chills. The extensive uses of oils, such as sesame, were one answer, and to balance their extreme tastes and effects, other ingredients — vinegar and salt, garlic and spring onions — were incorporated.

Spring onions appear in what is one of the Peking school's most representative styles — 'explosive cooking'. Dishes sautéed in wine or vinegar sauce are sizzled with water, coriander, bean paste and spring onions. Another noisy culinary glory of Peking are 'toffee' apples or bananas. The fruits are coated in a toffee-like syrup, which is swiftly dipped into iced water. The syrup solidifies to give crunchy coverings, with glorious results, similar to western toffee-apples, but so much better. Such desserts are typical of all 'Peking' food. Whether it is an hors d'oeuvre, main dish or dessert, a Peking speciality will be tasty, tender and crisp.

A BEAN CURD FACTORY near Peking run by soldiers of the People's Liberation Army.

The food of Shandong Province is a major element in Peking cuisine. The northern coast of the province has a large number of fisheries, and fish dishes predominate here. Fruit is more plentiful too, and the wines featured in so many Peking dishes are processed from the grapes grown at Chefoo and Tsingtao, the home of the internationally-exported Tsingtao beer, although the main Chinese wine is the yellow rice wine from Zhaoqin (formerly Shaohsing). Shandong is best known for its special stock, made from chicken, duck and pork.

There are other regional specialities, but Peking will remain best known for its Mongolian-based reminders of a distant nomadic age of cooking.

北京填鴨

鴨架白菜湯

北京填鴨

PEKING DUCK

1 duck (approximately
    2½-3kg/5-6lb)

Coating
1 tbsp malt sugar, honey or
    molasses
1 tsp cornflour
½ tsp vinegar

40-50 Chinese pancakes (see next
    recipe)
6 spring onions
1-2 red chillies

Sauce
2 tbsp hoisin sauce
1 tbsp peanut butter
1 tbsp sesame oil
1 tbsp Chinese yellow wine

Clean the duck, removing and discarding any excess fat in the cavity. Tie a piece of string around its neck. Pat dry.

Bring 4-5l (1 gallon) water to the boil and turn off the heat. Put the duck into the water and turn it backwards and forwards for about 1 minute. Remove. Bring the water to the boil again and repeat the previous step. Do this twice more (four times in all).

Hang the duck in a cool, draughty place for about 5 hours.

Mix the coating ingredients with 10 tbsp hot water and brush the duck all over with the mixture. Hang to dry for a further 4 hours and apply a second layer of coating.

Preheat the oven to 230°C (450°F/Gas Mark 8). Put a roasting pan in the oven with a wire rack in it, making sure that there is a space of about 5cm (2in) between the rack and the pan base.

Place the duck on the rack, breast side up, and roast for 8 minutes. Turn the duck over using a towel — not a fork — and roast for a further 8 minutes.

Reduce the temperature to 180°C (350°F/Gas Mark 4) and turn the duck breast side up again. Roast for 20 minutes. Lower the temperature to 130°C (250°F/Gas Mark ½) and roast for 10 minutes. Increase the heat again to 230°C (450°F/Gas Mark 8) and roast the duck for about 10 minutes. At this point you have to watch carefully to make sure that the skin of the duck does not burn. Turn off the heat once the skin has turned a rich deep red.

While the duck is roasting prepare the Chinese pancakes (see next recipe). Cut the spring onions into 5cm (2in) lengths, shred the tip of each piece and put it in iced water for 10 minutes. Decorate each piece with a red chilli ring.

Blend together the sauce ingredients over a low heat. Carve off the skin on the back of the duck. Hold the knife horizontally and carve the skin and meat from the breast and legs, cutting at an angle of 15°. Arrange the skin and meat on a large plate and serve it with pancakes, spring onions and the sauce.

Diners help themselves. They place one pancake flat on a plate, put a piece of duck in the centre, dip a spring onion in the sauce and put it on top of the duck, wrap it up and eat it.

PEKING DUCK (*On previous page*)
Many Chinese dishes are developments from a single ingredient to make maximum use of whatever is available. In this Pekinese selection, economy and variety are combined. The duck carcass, left over from Peking Duck, forms the basis of the soup, while the duck fat is used in the stir-fry to flavour the scrambled eggs. The shredded meat makes good use of meat leftovers, combined with vegetables which abound in all parts of China. The presentation of meat and crispy duck skin together is a play of contrasts between texture and flavour, unified by dipping them in the same sauce.

北京填鸭

CHINESE PANCAKES

½kg (1lb) plain flour
340ml (12fl oz/1½ cups) boiling
    water

1 tbsp sesame oil

Place the unsifted flour in a mixing bowl. Make a well in the centre and add the boiling water, stirring rapidly with a fork.

Knead the dough well on a lightly floured surface until it is smooth and firm. Return the dough to the mixing bowl, cover and leave to stand for 1 hour.

Knead the dough briefly on a lightly floured surface and roll into a sausage 3cm (1½in) in diameter. Pull it apart with your fingers to make about 40 equal-sized pieces. Roll the pieces between your hands to make smooth balls, making sure that they are all the same size.

Lightly oil the fingers and palms of your hands and flatten each ball until it is 4mm (¼in) thick. Brush the top with sesame oil.

Place one piece of dough on top of another, oiled sides facing, and roll out into a pancake 12-17cm (5-7in) across.

Heat the skillet and brush the bottom with sesame oil. Add the paired pancakes to the skillet one at a time. Cook over a medium heat for 30 seconds, turn and cook the other side for 30 seconds.

Pull the paired pancakes apart with your fingers to make two thin pancakes. Place them on a large piece of foil, one on top of the other, oiled side up.

Wrap them in the foil and steam for 30 minutes. Serve as an accompaniment to Peking Duck (see previous recipe). Any pancakes left over can be wrapped in foil and kept in the refrigerator for up to three days.

SCRAMBLED EGGS WITH ROAST DUCK FAT

5-6 tbsp roast duck fat from
    roasting pan of Peking Duck
4 tbsp chicken stock
2 tsp salt

¼ tsp pepper
6 eggs
1 tbsp minced ham
1 tbsp chopped coriander

In a mixing bowl mix 2-3 tbsp duck fat with the chicken stock, salt and pepper and the eggs.

Heat 2-3 tbsp of duck fat in a pan and add the egg mixture, beaten and well blended. Scramble over medium heat until set.

Remove and place on plate. Sprinkle with minced ham and chopped coriander and serve.

北
京
填
鴨

PEKING DUCK The duck is carved at table. White gloves are traditional.

A peeling action is used to remove the skin.

The knife is held horizontally.

The juicy meat is kept separate from the crispy skin.

The blade is held at an angle of 15°.

The meat is carved from the breast and legs.

Nothing is wasted.

When there is no more meat to carve, the beak is removed.

北京填鴨

PEKING DUCK
Spring onions, cucumber, pancakes and sweet sauce surround the carefully separated skin and meat. Peking duck is eaten in a distinctive way. The diner assembles his own pancakes, with some crispy duck skin, some meat (skin and meat are served separately), some chive or spring onion, and a generous dollop of sweet, plummy Peking duck sauce. The whole is then wrapped up. The contrast of textures and tastes is delicious.

Diners prepare their own pancakes.

Cucumber and spring onion are dipped in the sauce and placed on the pancake

... together with some duck meat and skin.

The rolled up pancake is ready to eat.

鴨
架
白
菜
湯

ROAST DUCK BONE, CABBAGE AND MUSHROOM SOUP

1 roast duck carcass (from Peking Duck)
1kg (2lb) Chinese cabbage
4-6 medium black mushrooms
1 tbsp peanut oil

½l (20floz/3 cups) chicken stock
900ml (32floz/4 cups) water
3-4 slices ginger
salt and pepper

Chop the duck bones into 7cm (3in) pieces and cut the Chinese cabbage into 5 × 7mm (2 × 3in) pieces.

Soak the black mushrooms in hot water for 30 minutes. Remove the stems.

Blanch the duck pieces in boiling water for 3 minutes. Remove.

Heat the peanut oil in a pan and stir-fry the Chinese cabbage for 2 minutes. Remove and set aside.

Bring the chicken stock and water to the boil. Add all the ingredients and simmer for 1½ hours. Season with salt and pepper to taste. Serve in a large bowl for diners to help themselves.

STIR-FRIED SHREDDED ROAST DUCK AND BEAN SPROUTS

300g (11oz) roast duck meat (from the back of the Peking Duck)
4-6 medium black mushrooms
3 tbsp peanut oil
2 tsp chopped ginger
1½ tsp chopped garlic
500g (1¼lb) bean sprouts

Sauce
1 tsp salt
1 tbsp light soy sauce
1 tsp sesame oil
1 tsp sugar
1 tbsp cornflour
4 tbsp stock
2-3 tbsp peanut oil

1 tsp Chinese yellow wine

Shred the roast duck meat.

Soak the black mushrooms in hot water for 30 minutes. Remove and discard the stems and cut the caps into shreds.

Heat 1 tbsp oil in a pan over high heat and add 1 tsp chopped ginger and ¾ tsp chopped garlic.

Add the bean sprouts, stir-frying over very high heat for 1 minute. Remove and set aside.

Heat 2 tbsp oil in the pan. Add the remaining ginger, garlic and the black mushroom shreds. Stir-fry for 30 seconds, add the roast duck and bean sprouts. Stir-fry briefly. Add the sauce ingredients, and stir rapidly over a very high heat for 30 seconds. Sprinkle with 1 tsp Chinese yellow wine and serve.

烙
韭
菜
盒

PAN-FRIED CHIVE AND DRIED SHRIMP CAKES

100g (4oz) plain four
6 tbsp cold water
50g (2oz) dried shrimps
500g (1¼lb) Chinese chives
4 tbsp peanut oil

1 tsp Chinese yellow wine
1 tbsp light soy sauce
2 tbsp shredded ginger
6 tbsp brown vinegar

Mix the flour and water in a bowl, first stirring with a fork, then kneading with your hands. Transfer the dough to a clean bowl, cover and leave to stand for 45 minutes.

Soak the dried shrimps in 4 tbsp hot water for 30 minutes before mincing them.

Chop the chives and set them aside.

Heat 3 tbsp oil in a pan. Add the shrimps and sauté for 30 seconds, then add the Chinese yellow wine, soy sauce and the chopped chives, stir and cook for 30 seconds. Remove from the pan and set aside.

Knead the dough for about 5 minutes until it is smooth. Roll it into a sausage shape and divide it into approximately 30 portions. Roll each piece into a ball. Flatten the dough with your hands and roll each one into a disc about 5cm (2in) across.

Put 1 tbsp chives and shrimps in the centre of each piece of dough and cover it with another piece. Seal the edges and place it on a lightly floured surface. Cover with a damp cloth. Repeat until all the dough is used up.

Place the cakes on lightly greased plates and steam over a high heat for 15 minutes. Remove and set aside.

Heat the pan and add 1 tbsp oil. Place the cakes in the pan and fry over low heat until golden in colour; turn over and fry the other side until golden. Serve with shredded ginger and brown vinegar.

SESAME SHRIMPS ON TOAST

40g (1½oz) pork fat
300g (11oz) shrimps, shelled and
  deveined
2 egg whites
¼ tsp pepper
1½ tsp salt

4 tbsp cornflour
1 tbsp chopped coriander
12 slices bread
1 egg yolk
2 tbsp sesame seeds
450ml (16floz/2 cups) peanut oil

Cook the pork fat in water for 3 minutes. Dice into small pieces.

Crush the shrimps with the flat side of a cleaver and place them in a mixing bowl with the pork fat, 1 egg white, ¼ tsp pepper, 1

烙
韭
菜
盒

PAN-FRIED CHIVE AND DRIED
SHRIMP CAKES
This is a luxury version of
the more standard onion
cakes. The cakes are
actually thickish pancakes
containing chives or
onion and garnished with
shrimp. The dough is
shallow-fried.

芝
蔴
蝦

SESAME SHRIMPS ON TOAST
This dish, usually eaten as a starter, is now quite often served in Chinese restaurants abroad. The shrimps are chopped, spread thickly on bread and deep fried. Sesame seeds are sprinkled on top, and the bread is served in chip-sized pieces.

STIR-FRIED SHRIMPS WITH PEAS
Restaurants often put too many peas into this dish, because they are cheaper than shrimps, but it is basically a shrimp dish. Coating the shrimp in a light egg white and cornflour batter and frying them briefly seals in the juiciness. Tomatoes, which are used here as a garnish, grow in great profusion around Peking in summer.

芝
蔴
蝦

tsp salt and 2 tbsp cornflour. Stir with a fork, in one direction only, until the mixture becomes consistent and sticky. Add the chopped coriander and stir. Set aside.

Trim the crusts from the bread and cut into slices 25 × 50 × 5mm (1 × 2 × ¼in). Mix 1 egg white with 1 tbsp cornflour and ½ tsp salt and brush the mixture on top of the bread slices.

Spread the shrimp mixture 1cm (½in) thick on the brushed side of the bread slices. Sprinkle sesame seeds on top, making sure that every piece is well covered. Mix the egg yolk with 1 tsp cornflour and brush the bottom of the bread slices with the mixture.

Heat the oil in a pan. Test the temperature with a thin slice of ginger: when the ginger turns slightly brown, add the shrimp bread, sesame side up. Fry over medium heat for 2 minutes and then turn over. Fry for a further 3 minutes over a lower heat. When nicely browned, turn over, increase the heat back to medium and fry for another 1-2 minutes.

Drain on a paper towel and serve hot.

STIR-FRIED SHRIMPS WITH PEAS

500g (1¼lb) shrimps	8 tbsp chicken broth
	1 tbsp cornflour mixed with 3 tbsp
Marinade	chicken stock
1 tsp salt	
1 egg white	50g (2oz) peas
1 tsp cornflour	½l (20fl oz/3 cups) peanut oil
	1 tsp salt
Sauce	1 tsp minced ginger
1 tbsp light soy sauce	1 tsp minced garlic
1 tsp sugar	1 tbsp Chinese yellow wine or dry
1 tsp sesame oil	sherry

Shell, devein and thoroughly rinse the shrimps; if they are too big, cut them into halves or thirds. Put the shrimps in a bowl and marinate in the refrigerator in a mixture of 1 tsp salt, 1 egg white and 1 tsp cornflour for 30 minutes.

Mix together the sauce ingredients, except for the cornflour.

Blanch the peas in 450ml (16fl oz/2 cups) water, plus 1 tbsp oil and 1 tsp salt for 2 minutes. Drain.

Heat 450ml (16fl oz/2 cups) oil, add the shrimps, stirring to separate, drain and set aside.

Heat 2 tbsp oil, add the minced ginger and garlic and when the aroma arises, add the shrimps and peas, stirring rapidly over a high heat.

Thicken the sauce mixture with the blended cornflour and add it to the pan. Add the yellow wine to the mixture and serve.

GRILLED KING PRAWNS PEKING STYLE

1kg (2lb) king prawns	2 tsp sugar
6 tbsp peanut oil	1 tsp salt
6 slices ginger	4 tbsp chicken stock
1 tsp garlic	1 tbsp shredded leek
2 tbsp Chinese yellow wine	1 tsp sesame oil

Trim the king prawns and devein them. Cut each in half but leave the shells on.

Heat the oil in a pan, add the ginger and garlic and, when the fragrance arises, sauté the king prawns for 2 minutes. Add the yellow wine, sugar, salt and chicken stock, reduce the heat and cook until the sauce has reduced to about one-third.

Add the shredded leek and the sesame oil and serve.

FISH ROLLS IN WINE SAUCE

500g (1¼lb) fillet of croaker or any white fish	2 tbsp peanut oil
1 egg white	**Sauce**
1 tsp cornflour	225ml (8floz/1 cup) chicken stock
2 medium black mushrooms	1 tsp lees of rice wine
40g (1½oz) ham	2 tsp sugar
150g (5oz) bamboo shoots	1 tsp salt
1kg (2lb) green cabbage	1 tsp sesame oil
2 spring onions	2 tbsp Chinese yellow wine
4-6 slices ginger	1½ tbsp cornflour

Cut the fillet of fish into slices 40 × 90 × 5mm (1¾ × 3½ × ¼in). Mix the egg white and cornflour, coat the fillets with the mixture and set them aside.

Soak the black mushrooms in hot water for 30 minutes. Cut off and discard the stems and cut the caps into fine shreds, 4cm (1¾in) long.

Cut the ham and the bamboo shoots into fine shreds, also 4cm (1¾in) long, and blanch the bamboo shoots in boiling water for 1 minute. (If you are using tinned bamboo shoots, blanching is not necessary.)

Place the shredded bamboo shoots, ham and mushrooms on the fish slices and roll them up. Each roll should have a diameter of 2-3 cm (¾-1½in).

Take the heart of the green cabbage and cut it in half. Blanch the cabbage in 1l (2 pints/5 cups) boiling salted water for 2 minutes. Remove and set aside.

Place 2 spring onions on a plate. Arrange the fish rolls and

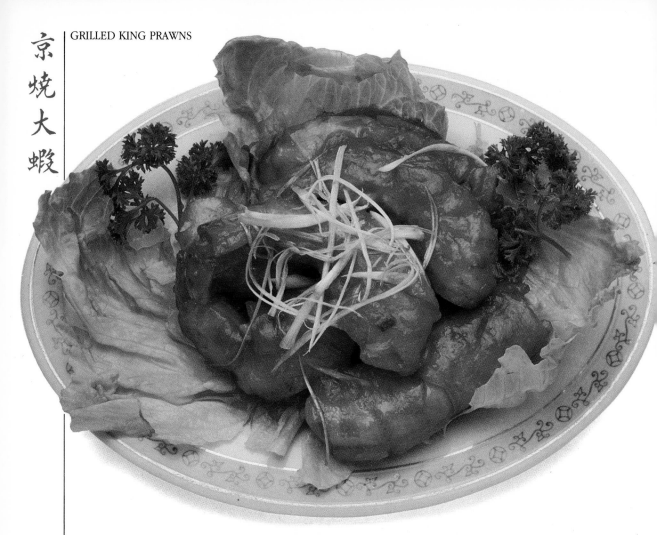

GRILLED KING PRAWNS PEKING STYLE
The name is a little misleading, because the prawns are actually fried. They are large and juicy and retain their flavour well when cooked in this way. They can be eaten as a starter or a main dish and go well with wine.

BRAISED CROAKER IN SOY SAUCE
Croaker is a meaty fish common in Hong Kong and the south-east of China. It is deep fried a little before the soy sauce is added, and ginger and spring onion are often used as flavourings. It is good eaten on its own or with rice.

糟溜魚卷

FISH ROLLS IN WINE SAUCE
Sole or plaice is good for this dish. The lightly battered fish is rolled around ham, asparagus or some other filling and poached in hot oil for a very short time before being cooked in wine sauce, sometimes with fish roes. The wine sauce is made from a concentrated wine, sugar and chicken stock.

CRISPY 'SQUIRREL' FISH
When the fish is scored on one side and deep fried, the tail curls up to look like a squirrel's tail. Usually served in sweet-and-sour sauce, this dish is popular in north China and along the Yangtze River.

ginger slices on top and garnish with the poached green cabbage. Steam over a high heat for 5-7 minutes.

Heat 2 tbsp peanut oil in a pan. Add the sauce ingredients, stir and bring to the boil. Pour over the fish rolls and serve.

BRAISED CROAKER IN SOY SAUCE

600-800g (1½-1¾lb) croaker, sea bass, turbot or pike	1 tbsp pork back fat, diced
2 medium black mushrooms	3 tbsp dark soy sauce
8 tbsp peanut oil	1½ tsp sugar
2 spring onions	170ml (6floz/¾ cup) chicken stock
3 slices ginger	1 tsp sesame oil

Clean the fish thoroughly, pat dry and set it aside.

Soak the mushrooms in hot water for 30 minutes. Remove and discard the stems and cut the caps into shreds.

Heat 6 tbsp oil in a pan. Add the spring onions and ginger, and remove and discard them when they have browned. Fry the fish for 30 seconds over a very high heat; turn it over and fry the other side for 30 seconds, still over very high heat.

Add the diced pork fat, soy sauce, sugar, chicken stock and black mushrooms to the pan, reduce the temperature and simmer over low heat for 30 minutes. Add 2 tbsp oil to the pan and increase the heat. Reduce the sauce to about half, add the sesame oil and serve.

CRISPY 'SQUIRREL' FISH

1½kg (3lb) croaker or sea bass	50g (2oz) wheat flour
	450ml (16floz/2 cups) peanut oil
	3 spring onions (white part only), cut into thin shreds
Marinade	
1 tsp salt	1 red chilli, finely shredded
1 tbsp light soy sauce	1 tbsp shredded ginger
1 tsp sugar	450ml (16floz/2 cups) sweet-and-
1 tsp Chinese yellow wine	sour sauce (see page 37)

Clean the fish. Remove the fillets from both sides, keep the head and tail but discard the backbone. Place the fillets, skin side down, on a chopping-board and score the flesh deeply to form a diamond pattern but do not cut through the skin.

Mix the marinade ingredients together and marinate the fish fillets. Coat the head and tail of the fish with wheat flour.

Heat the oil and fry the head and tail until nicely golden in

松
鼠
魚

colour. Remove and set aside. Coat the fillets of fish with wheat flour and fry over a medium heat until nicely golden. Remove and set aside.

Increase the heat, return the fish to the hot oil and fry for 15 seconds. Remove and drain. Arrange the fish neatly on a serving dish with the head, body and tail in one rounded curve`like a squirrel's tail. Place the spring onion, ginger and red chilli on top.

Bring the sweet-and-sour sauce to the boil, pour it over the fish and serve.

FISH IN WINE-LEE SAUCE

600g (1¹/₂lb) fillet of white fish such as sea bass, cod, turbot or halibut	**Sauce** 3 tsp rice wine or 2 tsp wine-lee paste if available
¹/₂ egg white	1 tsp salt
2 tsp cornflour	1¹/₂ tbsp sugar
3-4 wood-ear mushrooms (champignons chinoises)	225ml (8floz/1 cup) stock
450ml (16floz/2 cups) peanut oil	1 tbsp cornflour dissolved in 2 tbsp water

Cut the fish fillet into six pieces and mix it with the egg white and 2 tsp cornflour.

Soak the mushrooms in water for 30 minutes and cut them into small pieces.

Heat a pan until it is very hot. Pour in the peanut oil to heat for 20 seconds and add the sliced fish to fry for 15 seconds. Remove and drain away the oil. Add 1 tbsp peanut oil, the sauce, the fish and the mushrooms. Finally add the cornflour to the pan to thicken the sauce. Serve.

CHICKEN FU-YUNG

4 chicken breasts	**Sauce**
4 tbsp chicken stock	8 tbsp chicken stock
6 egg whites	¹/₂ tsp salt
1 tbsp cornflour	1 tbsp cornflour
1 tsp salt	2 tsp Chinese yellow wine
225ml (8floz/1 cup) peanut oil	
2 slices ginger	2 tsp ham, minced
1 garlic clove	2 tsp coriander leaves, finely chopped

Pound the chicken breasts with the back of a cleaver and mince the chicken meat finely. Add 2 tbsp chicken stock to the minced

木須肉

芙
蓉
雞
片

MU HSU PORK
Mu Hsu is a yellow-coloured flour, and this is a simple pancake dish that anyone can make. The shredded meat is scrambled with beaten egg and fresh or dried vegetables, including perhaps yellow tiger lily or black mushrooms. The savoury mixture is then spooned into a pancake and rolled up.

CHICKEN FU-YUNG
Shredded or minced chicken breast is deep-fried with beaten egg white. The bite-sized pieces are drained then cooked in stock thickened with cornflour. Wine may be added to the sauce.

FRIED FILLET OF PORK (*Far left*) The use of aromatic pepper in this dish makes it distinctively Pekinese. It is usually served with a dip.

meat and force the mixure through a sieve. Add 1 tbsp egg white to the sieved meat and stir well.

Blend 1 tbsp cornflour with 2 tbsp chicken stock. Mix the egg whites, salt and minced chicken together, stirring with a fork in one direction only, and add the blended cornflour, continuing to stir and mix the ingredients thoroughly.

Heat a pan until it is very hot and add the peanut oil. When the oil is warm, add tablespoonfuls of the egg white and minced chicken mixture. Reduce the heat to low and use a spatula to push the egg mixture to and fro in the pan. When it begins to set into snowflake-like pieces, remove them with a perforated spoon, drain and set them aside on a plate to keep warm.

Heat 2 tbsp oil in the pan. Add the ginger and garlic, but remove and discard them when they have turned brown.

Blend together the ingredients for the sauce, add to the pan and bring to the boil. Stir and pour over the egg white mixture.

Sprinkle the minced ham over the sauce and garnish with the chopped coriander leaves before serving.

MU HSU PORK

Seasonings
2 tsp light soy sauce
1/2 tsp sesame oil
1 tsp cornflour
1 tsp Chinese yellow wine

300g (11oz) pork
100g (4oz) dried tiger lily stems
50g (2oz) wood-ear mushrooms (champignons chinoises)

50g (2oz) bamboo shoots
4 tbsp peanut oil
1 tsp chopped ginger
3 tsp dark soy sauce
2 tsp sugar
6 eggs, lightly beaten
4 tbsp chicken stock
1 tbsp chopped spring onions
20 Chinese pancakes (see page 145)

Blend together the seasonings and add the pork, cut into match-stick-size shreds. Set aside.

Soak the dried tiger lily stems and the wood-ear mushrooms in hot water for 30 minutes. Cut away and discard any tough parts and chop the remainder into 3cm (1½in) pieces. Thinly slice the bamboo shoots.

Heat 2 tbsp oil in a pan and add the chopped ginger. When the aroma arises, add the pork and cook, stirring, for 1 minute. Add the tiger lily stems, bamboo shoots, wood-ear mushrooms. Add 1 tsp dark soy sauce and 1 tsp of sugar and cook for 1 minute, continuing to stir. Transfer to a plate and set aside.

Heat 2 tbsp oil in the pan and add the lightly beaten eggs, stirring gently with a spatula over medium heat. Cook until set and scrambled. Return the pork and vegetables to the pan and keep on stirring. Break the egg into pieces.

乾炸裏脊

Add the chicken stock, the remaining soy sauce and then the sugar, stirring rapidly over a very high heat for 1 minute, and the chopped spring onion. Serve with Chinese pancakes. To eat, place a pancake flat on the plate and spoon Mu Hsu pork on top. Roll up, fold one end over and eat from the open end.

FRIED FILLET OF PORK

Marinade
2 tsp Chinese yellow wine
1 egg white
1 tbsp cornflour
1 tbsp light soy sauce

500g (1¼lb) fillet of pork
1 tbsp salt
1 tbsp Sichuan peppercorns
450ml (16floz/2 cups) peanut oil

Mix together the ingredients for the marinade. Cut the fillet of pork into bite-size slices and marinate for 15-30 minutes.

Sauté the salt and peppercorns over a low heat for 2 minutes. Discard the peppercorns, transfer the salt to a saucer and set it aside for use as a dip.

Heat the oil in a pan until hot. Add the pork and lower the temperature. Simmer for 3 minutes. Turn off the heat and let the pork stand in oil for 5 minutes. Remove and drain.

Heat the oil again until very hot. Return the pork and stir-fry for 1-2 minutes, being careful not to burn it — it should be a nice golden colour, slightly crisp outside, but juicy inside.

Serve with peppery salt as dip.

PRECIOUS THINGS CASSEROLE

4-6 medium black mushrooms
4 tbsp peanut oil
3-4 slices ginger
50g (2oz) dried shrimps
250g (9oz) Chinese cabbage
900ml (32floz/4 cups) chicken
   stock

50g (2oz) bamboo shoots, sliced
50g (2oz) ham
50g (2oz) cooked chicken, sliced
50g (2oz) cooked shrimps
50g (2oz) abalone, sliced
2 tsp salt
1 tsp sesame oil

Soak the mushrooms in hot water for 30 minutes. Remove and discard the stems and set the caps to one side.

Heat the oil in a clay pot. Add the ginger slices, dried shrimps and Chinese cabbage cut into strips 1 × 7cm (½ × 3in) and cook for 2 minutes.

Add the chicken stock, bring to the boil and cook over a medium heat for 10 minutes. Add the sliced bamboo shoot, mushrooms and ham and continue to cook over a medium heat

PRECIOUS THINGS CASSEROLE

A hearty dish that is particularly warming in winter. The ingredients vary but are likely to include dried mushrooms, pork and chicken. Double-boiling makes the liquid very flavoursome.

EXPLOSIVE FRIED KIDNEY AND TRIPE WITH CORIANDER

This dish calls for careful timing, since overcooked kidney loses its crunch. It is unusual, however, for tripe to be cooked for such as short time.

AROMATIC MUTTON (*Bottom left*)

This is marinated lamb or mutton steamed and cooled then deep-fried until somewhat crisp.

DEEP-FRIED SMOKED SHREDDED CHICKEN (*Bottom right*)

Chicken is smoked on a wire platform in a pot, with rice, sugar and tea leaves at the bottom. The pot is heated and the smoke flavours the chicken.

STIR-FRIED MINCED BEEF WITH SICHUAN PICKLED VEGETABLES (*Opposite page*)

This is the Chinese version of the hamburger. The mustard greens give the beef a salty, vinegary flavour.

榨菜肉末

for 15 minutes. Finally add the cooked chicken, shrimps, abalone, salt and sesame oil. Serve.

If you increase the quantities you can make enough soup to last several meals. However, remember to keep the leftovers refrigerated.

AROMATIC MUTTON

600g (1½lb) fillet of muton	*1 tbsp cornflour*
Marinade	*300g (11oz) leeks*
1 tbsp light soy sauce	*450ml (16floz/2 cups) peanut oil*
1 tsp dark soy sauce	*1 tsp chopped garlic*
1 tsp sesame oil	*1 tsp Chinese yellow wine*
2 tsp Chinese yellow wine	

Cut the fillet of mutton into thin slices. Mix together the marinade ingredients, add the mutton slices and set to one side.

Cut the leek into thin slices and set aside.

Heat a pan until it is very hot and add the oil. Heat the oil until it is warm and add the mutton (reserving the marinade in a separate bowl) and stir to separate. Remove, drain and set aside.

Heat 2 tbsp oil in the pan and add the chopped garlic and leek, stir and cook over a very high heat for 1 minute.

Return the mutton to the pan, stirring well. Add the reserved marinade, stirring vigorously over a very high heat for 15 seconds. Finally, add the Chinese yellow wine, stir for another 10 seconds and serve.

EXPLOSIVE FRIED KIDNEY AND TRIPE WITH CORIANDER

4 pig's kidneys	*1 tsp chopped garlic*
2 tbsp salt	*50g (2oz) coriander, cut into 3cm*
2 pieces pork tripe	*(1½in) lengths*
2 tbsp cornflour	*1 tbsp light soy sauce*
8 tbsp chicken stock	*1 tsp Chinese yellow wine*
2 tbsp peanut oil	*1 tsp sesame oil*

Split the kidneys in half, remove the membrane and gristle and rub with 1 tbsp salt. Wash them thoroughly and leave them to soak in water for 30 minutes.

Split the tripe, rub it thoroughly with 1 tbsp salt. Wash and rub it vigorously with 2 tbsp cornflour. Make sure that it is completely clean. Set aside the thick part of the tripe (or you may prefer to cut off the outer skin on both sides). Score the tripe into a diamond pattern and cut it into slices 20 × 40 × 5mm (¾ × 1¾ × ¼in) using a cleaver with the blade held at an angle of 25°.

Cut up the kidney in the same way.

Bring the chicken stock to the boil and set it aside.

Heat the oil in a pan and add the garlic, tripe and kidney, stirring over a very high heat for 30 seconds. Add the coriander and hot chicken stock and bring to the boil. Drain off the stock and add the light soy sauce, Chinese yellow wine and sesame oil, stirfrying over a very high heat for 20 seconds. Serve.

Explosive frying involves cooking with very intense heat. It's a technique particularly suitable for ingredients with a delicate texture.

STIR-FRIED MINCED BEEF WITH SICHUAN PICKLED VEGETABLES

2 tbsp peanut oil	vegetable, minced
2 tsp chopped garlic	2 tbsp chicken stock
500g (1¼lb) beef, minced	1 tsp sugar
150g (5oz) Sichuan pickled	1 tbsp Chinese yellow wine

Heat 2 tbsp oil in a pan and add the garlic. When the aroma arises, add the minced beef, stirring over a high heat for 30 seconds.

Add the minced pickled vegetable and continue to stir and cook until the ingredients are dry. Add the stock, sugar and Chinese yellow wine to the pan and stir vigorously over a very high heat for 30 seconds. Transfer to a plate and serve with Sesame Cakes (see recipe below).

SESAME CAKES

450g (1lb) plain flour	1 tsp yeast
150g (5oz) lard	1 tbsp sesame oil
4 tbsp water	2 tbsp sesame seeds

Use a fork to mix half of the flour and lard with the water and yeast. Knead with your hands until the dough is smooth, cover and leave to stand for 30 minutes.

Make a second dough with the remaining flour and lard, again kneading with your hands until the dough is smooth. Set it aside.

Roll the first dough into a sausage shape and divide it into

乾
燒
二
鬆

DEEP-FRIED CONPOY AND
SHREDDED KALE
This dish is often called
Crispy Seaweed and is a
great favourite in Chinese
restaurants in the west.
The kale is cut into fine
shavings which are
double-deep-fried until
they are very crispy. These
are sprinkled with crispy
deep-fried and shredded
conpoy (dried scallops),
which provide an
evocative suggestion of
the sea.

PAN-FRIED ASPARAGUS IN EGG
BATTER
The asparagus is fried in a
small amount of oil with a
little chicken stock added
to allow longer cooking
time for the stalks.
Flavoured oil or chicken
fat with garlic and ginger
may be used, but any
stronger seasoning will
detract from the subtle
flavour of the asparagus.

SHARK'S FIN, HAM AND
CABBAGE SOUP
The emphasis here is on
the purity of the shark's
fin, which will already
have been through
several stages of cooking
before it reaches the clay
pot with the cabbage and
ham. The humble
cabbage makes a curious
contrast to the shark's fin,
a relatively luxurious item.

父
子
火
燒

approximately 24 pieces. Roll each piece into a ball. Repeat with the second dough, rolling it into a sausage and dividing it into approximately 24 pieces. Roll the pieces into balls but work them into cup shapes with your fingers. Put a ball made with the first dough inside each cup and wrap the cup around to form a large ball.

Roll the ball into a sausage between your palms and then use a rolling pin to roll each sausage into a long oval. Brush the top with oil.

Lay one oval on top of another, oiled sides facing, and press them together around the edges. Coat the top with sesame seeds and bake for 15-20 minutes at 180°C (350°F/Gas Mark 4).

To serve, cut the baked sesame cakes across the middle into two pouched pieces. Minced beef with pickled vegetables is spooned into the open ends of the cakes (or pouches) and they are eaten as a kind of sandwich.

DEEP-FRIED SMOKED SHREDDED CHICKEN

500g (1¼lb) chicken breasts	**Marinade**
1 tbsp tea leaves	*1 tbsp soya paste*
2 tsp sugar	*1 tsp light soy sauce*
1 tbsp cooked rice	*1 tsp Chinese yellow wine*
	½ tsp salt
	2 tbsp wheat flour
	450ml (16floz/2 cups) peanut oil

Steam the chicken breasts for 15 minutes. Heat a smoking pan and place in it the tea leaves, sugar and rice. Fit a rack into the pan and place the chicken on top. Cover the pan and when the pan is full of smoke, smoke the chicken for 5 minutes over medium heat.

Cut the chicken into strips 5 × 5 × 50mm (⅛ × ⅛ × 2in) and mix the chicken pieces with the marinade. Take the meat out of the marinade and coat the strips with wheat flour. Save the marinade.

Heat the oil in a pan and deep fry the chicken over medium heat until nicely golden. Take care when frying the chicken: turn off the heat immediately if you think the oil is getting too hot. Remove the chicken and drain.

Reheat the pan and return the chicken. Add the remaining marinade, stir vigorously over a high heat and serve.

If you use cooked chicken there is no need to steam the meat before smoking. In fact, cooked chicken is recommended since raw chicken seldom gives the crispiness that is one of the beauties of this lovely dish.

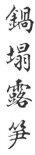

PAN-FRIED ASPARAGUS IN EGG BATTER

3 tbsp peanut oil
500g (1¼lb) asparagus
225ml (8floz/1 cup) chicken stock
1 tsp salt

2 eggs, lightly beaten
1 tbsp wheat flour
1 tsp Chinese yellow wine

Heat 1 tbsp oil. Add the asparagus (using only the tender spears), two-thirds of the chicken stock and the salt. Cook over a low heat until all the stock has evaporated and set aside.

Mix the eggs with the wheat flour in mixing bowl and thoroughly coat each asparagus spear with the egg batter.

Heat 2 tbsp oil in the pan, reduce the heat and arrange the asparagus, one by one, in the pan. Sauté gently for 1½ minutes. Turn the asparagus over and sauté for another 1½ minutes.

Add the remaining chicken stock, sauté until all the stock has evaporated and add the Chinese yellow wine. Sauté for 30 seconds and serve.

DEEP-FRIED CONPOY AND SHREDDED KALE

80g (3½oz) conpoy (dried
   scallops)
2 slices ginger
1 tsp Chinese yellow wine
150g (5oz) Chinese kale leaves or

pickled snow cabbage leaves
450ml (16floz/2 cups) peanut oil
2 tsp sugar
1 tsp salt

Soak the conpoy in water for 30 minutes. Add the ginger and Chinese yellow wine and steam for 15 minutes. Remove the conpoy, tear it into fine shreds and pat dry. Set it aside.

Cut the Chinese kale leaves into fine shreds, pat it dry and set aside. (If you are using pickled snow cabbage, soak it in 1l (40floz/5 cups) hot water for 30 minutes. Change the water and soak for another 30 minutes. Squeeze it dry, tear the leaves into small pieces and set them aside.)

Heat the peanut oil in a pan. Add the conpoy, stirring to separate, and fry until nicely golden in colour. Remove, pat dry with paper towels and set aside.

Add the kale or cabbage, again stirring to separate, and fry for 1 minute. Remove. If the vegetable is not crispy enough return it to pan for a short time. Remove and pat dry with paper towels.

Sprinkle 2 tsp sugar and 1 tsp salt over the vegetables and mix well. (If you are using pickled snow cabbage, there is no need to add salt.) Place the crispy vegetables on a plate, arrange the conpoy on top and serve.

涮羊肉

MONGOLIAN HOT-POT
The essence of this dish is a very rich stock which is made by dipping bundles of thinly sliced lamb into boiling water or stock. The meat is eaten as it is cooked, each person making up his own dipping sauce from a selection. When the meat is finished, the stock, with cabbage and noodles added, is drunk from the dip bowls.

TOFFEE APPLES
Small pieces of apple are coated in batter and deep fried. They are then coated again in molten rice sugar and quickly dipped in iced water so that the coating becomes cold and brittle, while the apple inside remains hot.

171

SHARK'S FIN, HAM AND CABBAGE SOUP

600g (1½lb) dried shark's fin (skin
and bone removed)
2 spring onions
50g (2oz) ginger
600g (1½lb) spare rib of pork
1.8l (64floz/8 cups) chicken stock

6 medium black mushrooms
6 tbsp peanut oil
6 slices ginger
600g (1½lb) cabbage
100g (4oz) ham, sliced

Prepare the shark's fin according to the recipe for Shark's Fin Consommé on page 40.

Bring 2l (4 pints) water to the boil. Add the spring onions, 50g (2oz) ginger and the shark's fin and simmer for 2 hours. Remove the shark's fin and set it aside.

Blanch the spare rib of pork in 1l (2 pints/5 cups) boiling water for 5 minutes. Rinse under the tap.

Bring the chicken stock and 900ml (32floz/4 cups) water to the boil. Add the spare rib of pork, simmer for 2 hours and set aside.

Soak the black mushrooms in hot water for 30 minutes. Cut off and discard the stems.

Heat the oil in a clay pot and add the ginger slices and cabbage, cut into strips 1 × 7cm (½ × 3in), stir and add the shark's fin. Place the mushrooms and ham slices on top, add the stock and bring to the boil. Simmer for 1 hour and serve.

MONGOLIAN HOT POT

1kg (2lb) lamb
4 cakes bean curd
4-6 Chinese dried mushrooms
500g (1¼lb) cabbage
500g (1¼lb) spinach
250g (9oz) bean-flour transparent
*   noodles*

Sauce
sesame oil
sesame paste

shrimp sauce
soy sauce
Chinese yellow wine
wine vinegar
sugar
chilli oil
fermented bean curd cheese
1 bundle chopped chives
chopped coriander leaves
4 stalks chopped spring onion

Cut the lamb into wafer-thin slices and arrange the slices on a large platter (or on several smaller plates to avoid stacking up slices of lamb). Cut each bean curd into eight or ten pieces.

Put plenty of water into the pot. Add the mushrooms and bring to the boil.

Diners are encouraged to mix their own sauce. One recipe would be to mix 1 tbsp each of sesame oil and sesame paste with 1 tsp each of shrimp sauce, light soy sauce, Chinese yellow wine and wine vinegar and ½ tsp sugar.

The more adventurous might care to add 1 tsp each of chilli oil and fermented bean curd cheese and chopped chives and stir in chopped coriander and spring onion.

Mix the sauce in a bowl, sample it and correct it to taste.

Pick up one or two slices of lamb at a time with chopsticks or put them in a small, long-handled wire basket, designed especially for this purpose. Cook the lamb very briefly in the boiling water in the hot pot. Transfer to the sauce bowl and eat.

Add the vegetables and bean curd half way through, and the bean-flour noodles towards the end, when the boiling water has turned into a rich soup after all the meat has been cooked in it. The contents of the hot pot should then be spooned or ladled out into the individual diner's bowl and drunk as a soup.

TOFFEE APPLES

3 apples
1 tbsp lemon juice
100g (4oz) cornflour
2 tbsp sesame seeds
1 cup ice cubes

½l (20 fl oz/3 cups) iced water
450ml (16 fl oz/2 cups) peanut oil
350g (12oz) sugar
1 tsp vinegar

Peel and core the apples and cut each into six pieces. Cut each piece into three. Sprinkle lemon juice over the apples immediately to prevent discoloration. Coat the apple pieces with cornflour and set them aside.

Sauté the sesame seeds in a pan over a low heat. Set aside.

Rub a serving plate with oil and set it aside. Place the ice cubes and iced water in a bowl and set them aside.

Heat the oil and fry the apple for 10 minutes until nicely golden. Remove, drain and set aside.

In another pan bring 340ml (12 fl oz/1½ cups) water to a vigorous boil. Add the sugar, stirring until it starts to caramelize, then add the vinegar and stir.

Add the apple pieces until they are evenly coated with syrup. Sprinkle sesame seeds over the apple and transfer them to a serving plate.

Dip the syrup-coated apple pieces into the iced water. Remove immediately or when the syrup hardens and becomes brittle. It is worth practising this recipe a few times to achieve the correct contrast between the brittle, ice-cold coating of caramelized sugar and the hot, tender apple centre.

WESTERN SCHOOL

South-western China's Sichuan Province is the most heavily populated region in China. Set about by high mountains, it stays warm in winter and gets very hot in the summer. The province's quarter of a million square miles of mostly mountainous territory rise in the west to the lofty Tibetan plateau. A land of mountains and mists, Sichuan is nevertheless a fruitful region, for the Yangtze River runs across it, and the heart of the province is the Red Basin. In its rich lands both the people and the farms are fertile — the population density is very high and the crops include rice, maize, sugar-cane, beans and tobacco.

Ancient irrigation systems and intense cultivation ensure that three crops of rice can be harvested annually. The irrigation schemes, which channel the converging waters of four rivers, are one indication of the independent power that the Sichuanese once had. Many marvellous Buddhist ruins and monuments are

further evidence of what was, until fairly recently, a proud kingdom.

Virtually inaccessible, because of those mountan ranges, Sichuan was not brought into contact with the outside, northern Chinese world until the reign of Kublai Khan in the thirteenth century, and local rulers maintained more than titular control for many centuries after. Thus Sichuan cuisine is quite distinct from other Chinese regional cooking schools. It can be divided into two basic types. The food of the peasants, in the countryside of the Red Basin, is the type the outside world now knows best. It is hot and fiery, heavily spiced with chilli, truly thrilling fare. Good, home-cooking style Sichuan food will have peppery, hot chilli-laden dishes, which, nevertheless, can never be confused with westernized Indian food, with its lashings of curry powder. Home-style Sichuan food can have a great subtlety and variety of fiery flavours.

The other main Sichuan cooking style arose among the ruling class and reflected external Chinese influences. Less hotly spiced, Sichuan banquet dishes are even subtler pleasures.

The province's geographical isolation from the rest of China did not mean that it was cut off from the outside world. In many ways Sichuan looked south for its culinary influences, and its fiery accent is part of a widespread culinary language that developed

BAMBOO SHOOTS, one of Sichuan's treasures (opposite).

KUNMING LAKE, Yunnan Province (middle).

A HOUSE IN CHENGDU is surrounded by bamboo groves (below).

TEA-PICKING in the Puer region of Yunnan, near the Burmese border. This strong black tea is considered good for a hangover.

all the way from India, through Burma and Thailand and across to Indo-China. Indeed, the people of Sichuan are related to their southern neighbours both racially and culturally. The Thais, for instance, are generally believed to have originated in this south-western region of China, moving south from Sichuan and its southern provincial neighbour of Yunnan. Even now there is a major Thai-speaking tribe living in the Sichuan region, along with sizeable populations of other minorities that are also found in Thailand and Indo-China's hill-tribe areas.

Buddhism was brought north from India two thousand years ago. Traders soon followed the missionaries, as they have in any religious movement, bringing with them both the spices and the cooking concepts of India. Spices and herbs were adopted both as medicines and cooking ingredients.

There are many theories why Sichuan Province has used chillies more than other areas in China. One story claims that the chilli was the only crop easily grown in the isolated mountain communities and was therefore used to help preserve foodstuffs. There may be some truth in the story, but it does not explain why the whole region, including its most fertile areas, adopted the chilli with such alacrity. It is more likely that the chilli proved its value as an antidote to the region's high humidity, for humidity tends to dull the appetite. Chilli not only stimulates the appetite, it increases the ability of the palate to appreciate various tastes.

Do not imagine that a Sichuan chilli is anything like a normal capsicum. Sichuan's glorious little chillies are culinary fire-bombs, which the Sichuanese fry to increase their explosiveness.

But, as in classic Indian cuisine, a cook does not rely on just one spice. His stock of taste enhancers and appetite stimulators includes brown peppercorns, ginger, garlic and onions. Sichuan cuisine, in fact, is famous for its refined and meticulous cooking styles and seasoning methods, which can create a palate-exciting variation of tastes within a single dish.

'Fish aroma' dishes are special delights. The 'fish aroma' is a special sauce flavoured with vinegar, wine lees, garlic, ginger, pepper, spring onion and the ever-faithful broad-bean paste. There is no trace of fish in the sauce.

Another outstanding Sichuan flavour is equally wrongly named. It is called 'queer taste'. But don't be misled by the name for there is nothing queer about dishes flavoured with it. The sauce is a perfect blend of a Sichuan cook's five key flavours — sweet, sour, salty, peppery and, of course, chillied. 'Queer taste chicken' is an especially famous dish, best enjoyed with spirits.

Other elements in a Sichuan dish include bitter flavours and distinctive aromatic and fragrant qualities. Sichuan cuisine places much less emphasis on side sauces: each dish is designed to provide its own textural and taste contrasts. Stir-fried dishes are cooked to the point where juices are almost entirely reduced .

Smoked duck is a Sichuan speciality. Even a connoisseur has difficulty in identifying a dominant factor, for the duck is seasoned with a variety of ingredients — ginger, orange peel, cinnamon, peppercorns and coriander — and then marinated in Chinese rice wine. After an initial steaming, the duck is smoked over a charcoal fire sprinkled with chips of camphor wood and red-tea leaves. The bird's final flavour and aroma are a heavenly blend of fascinating contrasts.

Sichuan food also incorporates dishes adopted from the neighbouring provinces of Hupei, Hunan and Yunnan, the last of which is particularly famed for its ham. However, each province has distinct characteristics. Yunnan is the odd man out among the Indo-Chinese areas because Kublai Khan's successors deliberately settled many Muslim Mongolians in the border territory. Just as the 'colonies' of Han Chinese had previously taken Peking practices out into the provinces, so did the Muslims in Yunnan.

Back to Sichuan for a momentary vote of thanks to the ubiquitous bean curd. The protein-rich soya bean features in many regional cuisines, and some of its finest versions can be found in Sichuan fare. The long Buddhist influence explains the Sichuan glories, but it is not necessary to be a vegetarian to appreciate the splendid versatility of bean curd in all its forms, whether it is as soft as an egg custard, cake-like, dried or frozen.

One seventeenth-century Chinese gentleman considered that one piece of advice about bean curd had to be passed on to his son. So he put it in his will, charging the son to remember that dried bean curd should be eaten with fried peanuts to savour the taste of the finest ham. Another writer claimed that good bean curd was a finer experience than bird's nest (a rare treat).

The same writer also sang the praises of bamboo shoots, another of Sichuan's treasures. Bamboo is one dish that must be prepared without any potentially overwhelming companions, and enjoyed by itself with just a trace of flavour from pickled vegetable or dried shrimp roe. The poet Su Shih wrote that he would prefer to take a meal without meat rather than live in a place without bamboos. 'Without meat a man can grow thin', he noted. 'Without bamboo he will grow vulgar', he added.

However, understanding the subtlety of Sichuan food is not that simple. It is China's boldest food and perhaps the only one that shows off external non-Chinese influences. Proudly different from mainstream Chinese cooking styles, it recalls an age of Sichuan independence.

MAO TAI, the spirit made from the grain of these sorghum plants, is 110° proof, stronger than pure Russian vodka. It is a speciality of Guizhou.

BRAISED CROAKER

BRAISED CROAKER IN CHILLI SAUCE
The fish is deep fried then cooked in a chilli sauce made from fresh or dried chillies and soy bean paste. Browned pork with ginger and spring onion are used to intensify the flavour.

PRAWNS IN SICHUAN SAUCE
The prawns are fried then cooked with other ingredients such as bamboo shoots or diced aubergine in a pre-mixed hot sauce, which consists of chopped chilli and garlic in soy paste. Wine and sugar can also be added.

酸
辣
湯

SOUR AND PEPPERY SOUP
Usually called hot-and-sour soup, this is popular everywhere. A strong savoury soup stock is made adding fresh chicken or shrimp and chopped bean curd. Then a thickened sauce with pepper, soy sauce and plenty of vinegar is combined with the stock.

SICHUAN DUMPLINGS IN RED SAUCE
The dumplings are made by steaming or poaching minced pork wrapped in a thin skin of dough. The sauce is actually red oil made by soaking dried chilli peppers in oil overnight.

BRAISED CROAKER IN CHILLI SAUCE

600-800g (1½-1¾lb) croaker, sea
  bass, turbot or pike
2 tbsp cornflour
10 tbsp peanut oil
2 tsp chopped garlic
1 tbsp chopped spring onion
1 red chilli, cut into small rings

1 tbsp chilli broad bean paste (flat
  bean paste)
1 tbsp soy bean paste
1 tsp·vinegar
1 tsp sugar
225ml (8floz/1 cup) chicken stock
2 tsp Chinese yellow wine

Clean the fish thoroughly, pat it dry and lightly coat with cornflour. Heat 8 tbsp oil in pan. Fry the fish over a very high heat for 2
minutes on each side. Remove and set aside.

Heat 2 tbsp oil in a pan. Add the garlic, spring onion and chilli,
and stir. Add the chilli broad bean paste, soy bean paste, vinegar
and sugar, stirring. When the aroma rises, add the chicken stock.
Stir to mix well. Return the fish to pan, cover it up, and cook over
medium heat for approximately 10 minutes.

Add 2 tbsp oil around the edge of the fish. Increase the heat,
and add the Chinese yellow wine. Garnish with chopped coriander and serve.

PRAWNS IN SICHUAN SAUCE

500g (1¼lb) king prawns,
  trimmed and deveined
3½ tbsp peanut oil
2 tsp yellow wine
2 tbsp chicken stock
1 tbsp Sichuan hot bean paste
½ tbsp chopped Sichuan pickle

2 tsp chopped ginger
1 tsp salt
large pinch scallion
8 tbsp chicken broth
1 tbsp tomato sauce
½ tsp chilli oil or sauce

Cut each prawn into three equal parts. Heat the pan for 10
seconds and add 2 tbsp oil. Stir-fry the prawns in the hot oil for 1
minute over a high heat. Add the wine and chicken stock, cover
and allow to cook for 1 minute. Remove from heat.

Heat 1½ tbsp peanut oil in a pan. Add the bean paste, pickle,
ginger, salt, scallion and chicken broth. Stir together for 30
seconds. Add the prawns and continue to stir-fry over moderate
heat for 1 minute. Add the tomato sauce and chilli oil or sauce and
stir-fry once more over high heat. Serve.

SOUR AND PEPPERY SOUP

20g (¾oz) black mushrooms
40g (1½oz) chicken blood
  pudding

20g (¾oz) sea cucumber
20g (¾oz) cooked chicken or ham
20g (¾oz) squid

酸
辣
湯

40g (1½oz) bean curd
20g (¾oz) cooked pork
1 tsp light soy sauce
1 tsp dark soy sauce
1 tsp pepper
1 tsp chilli oil
½l (20fl oz/3 cups) chicken stock

2 tbsp cornflour, blended with 2
  tbsp water
1 egg, lightly beaten
2 tsp spring onion, choppd
2 tsp brown vinegar
1 tsp sesame oil

Soak the black mushrooms in hot water for 30 minutes; remove and discard the stems and cut the caps into shreds.

Shred the blood pudding, sea cucumber, chicken meat (or ham), squid, bean curd and cooked pork, and add to the soy sauces, pepper and chilli oil in a pan. Add the shredded mushroom and the chicken stock and bring to the boil. Stir in the softened cornflour and the egg.

Place the spring onions, brown vinegar and sesame oil in a soup tureen, pour the soup into the tureen and serve.

SICHUAN DUMPLINGS IN RED SAUCE

4 medium black mushrooms
250g (9oz) fillet of pork
100g (4oz) pork fat
100g (4oz) chives or white of
  spring onion
2 egg whites
2 tbsp cornflour
1 tsp salt
1 tsp sesame oil
40 wonton wrappers

Red sauce
2 tbsp sesame oil
1 tbsp chilli oil
1 tbsp chopped garlic
1 tsp Sichuan peppercorn powder
2 tbsp sesame paste
2 tbsp dark soy sauce
1 tbsp chopped young leeks or
  spring onions
2 tsp sugar

Soak the black mushrooms in hot water for 30 minutes. Remove and discard the stems. Set aside.

Finely dice the fillet of pork and the pork fat and chop the chives or the white of the spring onions into tiny pieces.

Place the pork, mushrooms and chives in a mixing bowl. Add 1 egg white, 1 tbsp cornflour, 1 tsp salt and 1 tsp sesame oil and mix well.

Put 1 tbsp of the pork mixture in the centre of a wonton wrapper. Mix the other egg white with 1 tsp cornflour and wet two of the edges of the wrapper. Fold up the wrapper diagonally to form a triangle and press the edges to seal. Fold two opposite corners over and stick together with more of the egg white and cornflour mixture.

In a large pan boil 3l (6 pints) water and add the dumplings. When they float to the surface, add 225ml (8fl oz/1 cup) cold water and bring back to the boil again. Remove and drain the dumplings, arranging them in a medium-size serving bowl (six dumplings to each bowl). Prepare the red sauce and serve.

肝
蒸
湯

CHICKEN LIVER MOUSSE CLEAR SOUP

Either chopped chicken liver or chicken blood can be used. It is steamed until set then chopped into diamond-shaped or triangular pieces which are added to the soup during cooking. For a livelier taste, chilli can be added either to the livers beforehand or to the soup itself.

STIR-FRIED CHICKEN KUNG-PO STYLE

Chicken is diced into cubes, coated in cornflour and stir-fried, first in very hot oil, then with the oil drained off. Kung-po style means the dish is coloured pink with a combination of soy sauce and red oil, which gives it a distinctive flavour and appearance.

MULTI-FLAVOURED CHICKEN
The particular flavour of
this dish comes from the
addition of sesame sauce
to the sauce during
cooking.

SMOKED DUCK SICHUAN STYLE
Smoke from sugar and tea
burned together
permeates the previously
braised duck meat to
flavour it. The whole
duck is placed on a wire
rack in a pot with a lid
and the mixture is heated
inside the pot until it
smokes. After cooling, the
duck can be deep-fried
and eaten with a dipping
sauce.

川椒鷄球

STIR-FRIED CHICKEN KUNG-PO STYLE

500g (1¼lb) breast of chicken	2 tsp cornflour

Seasoning
1 tsp sugar
1 tbsp dark soy sauce
1 tbsp cornflour

Sauce
1 tsp sugar
2 tsp vinegar
1 tbsp dark soy sauce
3 tbsp stock

4 tbsp peanut oil
1 tsp peppercorns
1 tsp dried red chilli, cut in ring
   form
1 tsp Chinese yellow wine or dry
   sherry
3 slices ginger
1 tsp chopped garlic
2 tsp chopped scallion
100g (4oz) roasted peanuts

Cut the chicken into cubes (1cm/½in) and mix the meat with the seasoning ingredients.

In a separate bowl, blend together the ingredients for the sauce and set it to one side.

Heat the oil in a pan add the peppercorns and dried red chilli and when the chilli darkens in colour, pour the oil into a bowl through a strainer. Discard the peppercorns.

Return the oil and the dried red chilli to the pan, and add the chicken. Stir-fry for 1 minute, add the yellow wine, then the ginger, garlic and scallion. Keep on stirring and turning the ingredients. Add the sauce ingredients, stir well, then add the roast peanuts. Stir and serve.

A variation of this spicy, full-flavoured dish is given in the recipe below.

CHICKEN WITH SICHUAN CHILLI

400g (14oz) fresh breast of chicken
2 tsp shrimp sauce
1 tsp dark soy sauce
1 tsp cornflour
3½ tsp Chinese yellow rice wine or
   sherry
450ml (16floz/2 cups) peanut oil
40g (1½oz) pearl leaves (finely

shredded leaves of Chinese kale
   or mint are a good substitute)
1 tsp chopped spring onion
½ tsp Sichuan peppercorns
½ tsp monosodium glutamate
   (optional)
3-4 drops sesame oil

Cut the chicken into slices 5mm (¼in) thick and pound the meat to tenderize it. Mix the chicken with 1 tsp shrimp sauce, 1 tsp dark soy sauce, 1 tsp cornflour and 1½ tsp rice wine.

Heat a pan until it is very hot and add the oil. When hot, fry the chicken until it is almost cooked but do not let the oil boil. Remove the chicken from the pan to drain.

Fry the vegetable leaves in hot oil over a high heat for 75

seconds. Remove them from the pan, drain thoroughly and arrange them around the edge of a plate to keep warm.

Heat the pan again until it is very hot. Add 1 tbsp oil. Fry the spring onion until fragrant, add the peppercorns and then the chicken. Add 1 tsp shrimp sauce, ½ tsp monosodium glutamate (if used), 3-4 drops sesame oil and 2 tsp rice wine and sauté for a short while over high heat. Remove and place in the centre of the plate surrounded by the stir-fried vegetable.

CHICKEN LIVER MOUSSE CLEAR SOUP

225g (8oz) chicken liver
5 egg whites
1 egg yolk
900ml (32floz/4 cups) chicken
   stock

1 tsp salt
2 tsp Chinese yellow wine
¼ tsp pepper
½ tsp sesame oil

Finely mince the chicken livers and run them through a sieve.

Add the 5 egg whites and the egg yolk to 340ml (12floz/1¼ cups) chicken stock. Stir to mix well together in a basin. Add the salt, yellow wine, pepper and sesame oil, stir and blend thoroughly.

Grease the bottom of a medium-sized soup tureen and transfer the mixture to it to steam over medium heat until set, which will take 7-8 minutes.

Heat the remaining chicken stock and place it in a large soup tureen. Transfer the chicken liver mousse to the large tureen, taking care not to damage the mousse in the transfer. Serve for eating throughout the meal.

SMOKED DUCK SICHUAN STYLE

1½kg (3lb) duck
1½ tsp peppercorns
2 tbsp salt
2 tbsp jasmine tea
1 tbsp sugar

½ tsp pepper powder
2 tbsp Chinese yellow wine or dry
   sherry
900ml (32floz/4 cups) peanut oil
1 tbsp sesame oil

Clean the duck and soak it in 4l (8 pints) water with peppercorns and salt added for 4 hours.

Blanch the duck in boiling water for 5 minutes. Dry thoroughly.

Heat a dry pan over moderate heat, add 2 tbsp jasmine tea, 1 tbsp sugar and cover with a lid. After 1 minute, place a wire rack in the pan and lay the duck on the rack. Replace the lid firmly and

DOUBLE-COOKED PORK

A very popular dish that
is easy to prepare. Belly
of pork is usually
preferred by the Chinese,
as it has more fat. The
meat is boiled, sliced and
cooked again in a hot
savoury sauce thickened
with red oil or tomato
paste, which gives it a
pleasing colour and taste.

SLICED PORK WITH GARLIC
SAUCE

This Sichuan dish is also
very popular in Peking,
where garlic is used
liberally. Its appeal lies in
its simplicity. Boiled belly
or shoulder of pork is
sliced very thinly then
sprinkled with minced
garlic, by itself or stirred
into a light soy sauce.

芹黃牛肉麵

MINCED BEEF, CELERY, CHIVES
AND NOODLES IN SOUP
The proper name for this
typical Sichuan dish is
Dan-Da noodles. It
consists of noodles in a
clear stock with stir-fried
beef in a savoury sauce
placed on top so that the
flavour and hotness
permeate the noodles and
liquid.

smoke the duck for about 10 minutes over low heat and then leave to stand in the smoke until it turns light golden brown.

Rub the duck all over with pepper powder and Chinese yellow wine and steam for 2 hours. Set aside.

Heat 900ml (32fl oz/4 cups) peanut oil in a deep pan. When hot, add the duck and deep fry until the skin is rich golden brown and crispy.

Take the duck out of the pan and brush with sesame oil. Chop into bite-size pieces and serve.

MULTI-FLAVOURED CHICKEN

2kg (4-5lb) fresh chicken

Sauce
2 tbsp sesame oil
1 tsp brown vinegar
1 tsp sugar

1 tbsp chilli sauce
1 tbsp chopped garlic
1 tsp ground peppercorns
3 tbsp shredded spring onions
1½ tsp salt
8 tbsp stock

Clean the chicken thoroughly.

Put 1.25l (48fl oz/6 cups) water into a pan and bring to the boil. Add the chicken and simmer for 10 minutes over low heat. Remove the chicken and rinse under the tap for 2 minutes. Return the chicken to the water and boil for 5 minutes. Rinse with cold water again.

Remove the bones from the chicken and hand-shred the meat, arranging the shredded chicken on a plate.

Blend together the ingredients for the sauce. Pour it over the chicken on the dish and serve.

SLICED PORK WITH GARLIC SAUCE

2 stalks spring onions
6 slices ginger
500g (1¼lb) shoulder of pork
2 tbsp peanut oil
1 tsp Sichuan peppercorns
1 tbsp chopped garlic

1 tsp chopped spring onions
1 tbsp dark soy sauce
4 tbsp chicken stock
1 tsp sesame oil
1 tsp sugar
1 tsp chilli oil

Bring 2l (4 pints/10 cups) water to the boil. Add one of the spring onions and the ginger and pork and cook for 30 minutes. Remove the pork from the pan and rinse it under the tap. Return it to the water and cook over medium heat for another 30 minutes.

Take out the pork again, rinse it under the tap, pat dry and cut into wafer-thin slices. Arrange on a plate and set aside.

Heat 2 tbsp oil in a pan and add the peppercorns. When they change colour, take them out of the pan and discard. Add the garlic and remaining spring onion stalk (cut into 1cm/½in sections) and sauté for 15 seconds. Add all the other ingredients, stir and mix well. Pour the mixture into a bowl and serve the pork with this sauce so that diners may dip the slices of meat in it.

A simple but tasty cold cut. An excellent starter to alert your palate for more exciting spicy dishes to follow.

DOUBLE-COOKED PORK

500g (1¼lb) belly of pork	*1 tbsp yellow bean paste*
4 tbsp peanut oil	*2 tsp dark soy sauce*
1 tsp salt	*100g (4oz) garlic leaves, cut into*
1 tbsp chilli bean paste or Sichuan	* 5cm (2in) lengths*
* tou pan jiang*	

Cook the pork in ½l (20floz/3 cups) boiling water for 20 minutes. Rinse the meat for 1 minute under the tap and then cut it into slices (50 × 30 × 4mm/2 × 1½ × ¼in).

Heat the oil in a pan over medium heat, add the pork slices and stir-fry for 10 seconds. Add the salt and continue to stir until the pork pieces curl up.

Add the chilli bean paste and the yellow bean paste and continue to stir. Finally, add the soy sauce and garlic leaves. Stir-fry for 10 seconds and serve.

MINCED BEEF, CELERY, CHIVES AND NOODLES IN SOUP

250g (9oz) Chinese celery	*500g (1¼lb) minced beef*
250g (9oz) Chinese white chives or	*2 tsp chopped spring onions*
* the white part of leeks*	*2 tsp chopped root ginger*
500g (1¼lb) dried white wheat	*2 tsp chopped Sichuan pickle*
* flour thick noodles*	*1 tbsp dark soy sauce*
500ml (18floz/2¼ cups) chicken	*2 tsp chilli oil*
* stock, boiling*	*2 tsp Sichuan peppercorn powder*
4 tbsp peanut oil	*4 tbsp chicken stock*

Chop the celery and white chives or leeks into shavings. Set aside.

Bring 2l (4 pints/10 cups) water to the boil and add the noodles. Reduce the heat to medium and cook for 5-6 minutes. Transfer the noodles to a large pan of cold water, stirring to keep them separate. Drain the noodles and return them to a pan of

DRY-FRIED CRISPY BEEF

DRY-FRIED CRISPY BEEF
The long frying time of
the Sichuan dry-frying
technique means that the
beef is really dry and
crisp, providing a
pleasant contrast of
texture to rice and other
ingredients such as spring
onions.

DRY-FRIED BEEF, FLAVOURED
WITH AGED ORANGE PEEL
The beef can be prepared
in two ways, either
stewed or crisp-fried with
sauce. Either way, the
flavour comes from
shredded orange or
tangerine peel.

SESAME BEEF
Sesame seeds, used
extensively in Sichuan
cooking, are heated in a
dry pan to bring out their
aromatic flavour and
added to dry-fried minced
beef. Chilli is often added
too.

乾煸牛肉絲

boiling water and cook for a further 2 minutes. Test with your fingers to see if they are cooked: they should be firm but also soft and easy to break. When they are cooked remove and drain them and divide them among four or six bowls.

Add 450ml (16floz/2 cups) of boiling chicken stock to the noodles in the bowls.

Heat the oil in a pan, add the minced beef and stir-fry quickly over high heat. Add the chopped celery and chives and, continuing to stir, cook for 30 seconds.

Add the remaining ingredients, including an additional 4 tbsp chicken stock, stir and bring the contents to the boil. Ladle over each bowl of noodles and serve one bowl to each diner.

DRY-FRIED BEEF, FLAVOURED WITH AGED ORANGE PEEL

600g (1½lb) lean beef (topside, tenderloin, etc.)	½l (20floz/3 cups) peanut oil
1 dried, aged orange or tangerine peel	½ tsp salt
	1½ tbsp sugar
3 slices root-ginger	1½ tbsp dark soy sauce
2 green chilli peppers	1 tbsp hoisin sauce
2 dried red chilli peppers	2 tbsp good stock
2 stalks spring onion	2 tbsp Shaohsing rice wine or dry sherry
6 tbsp cornflour	1½ tsp sesame oil
1 egg, lightly beaten	

Shred the beef into pieces the size of a 'double matchstick'. Wash and drain the pieces thoroughly.

Soak the dried orange or tangerine peel in warm water for 20 minutes and cut it into matchstick-size shreds. Cut the ginger and the green and red chilli peppers into similar size pieces and the spring onion into 5cm (2in) sections.

Mix together the cornflour and lightly beaten egg and coat the shredded beef, making sure that each piece is evenly covered.

Heat the oil in a pan or wok and, when a crumb dropped into the oil will sizzle, add the beef. Using a fork or wooden chopstick to separate the shreds, stir-fry the beef over a medium heat for 6-7 minutes. Remove the beef from the pan with a perforated spoon and set it aside to drain. Meanwhile, allow the oil in the pan to increase in temperature until it is smoking. Return the beef and stir-fry for a further 2 minutes. Remove the beef with a perforated spoon and drain thoroughly.

In a separate pan or wok heat 3 tbsp oil. When the oil is hot, add the shredded ginger, orange or tangerine peel and green and red chilli peppers and the spring onion pieces. Stir-fry them together for 1 minute before adding the salt, sugar, soy sauce, hoisin sauce, stock and wine. Continue to stir and cook for another minute, by which time the liquid should have reduced by about half. Return the beef to the pan and stir well to mix the ingredients together for 1 minute. Sprinkle the sesame oil over the mixture and serve.

SESAME BEEF

300g (11oz) rump steak

Marinade
1 tbsp light soy sauce
1 tsp dark soy sauce
1 tsp sugar

1 tsp sesame oil
1 tsp Chinese yellow wine

1 tbsp white sesame seeds
¹/₂l (20fl oz/3 cups) peanut oil

Cut the steak into thin slices (30 × 50 × 2mm/1¹/₂ × 2 × ¹/₈in). Prepare the marinade and mix the beef slices with it. Set aside.

Sauté the sesame seeds in a pan over a low heat until they are nicely golden in colour. Set aside.

Heat the peanut oil. Add the beef, reduce the heat to medium and fry for 3 minutes. Remove the meat and bring the oil back to a high temperature. Return the beef to the oil and fry for a further 30 seconds.

Drain the beef and pat it with a paper towel before transferring it to a serving dish. Sprinkle it with sesame seeds and serve.

DRY-FRIED CRISPY BEEF

450g (1lb) rump steak
100g (4oz) carrot
1 Chinese celery
4 tbsp peanut oil
3 tsp Chinese yellow wine

Seasoning
2 tsp chilli bean paste
1 tbsp hoisin sauce

2 tsp chopped garlic
2 tsp chopped spring onion
1 tsp sesame oil
1 tsp salt

1 tbsp sugar
1 tbsp chopped spring onion
1 tsp chopped ginger
¹/₂ tsp Sichuan peppercorn powder

Cutting across the grain, thinly slice the beef and then further cut it into 2mm (¹/₈in) shreds. Set aside.

Cut the carrot and celery into similar tiny pieces and set aside.

Heat a pan until it is very hot and add the oil. When the oil is hot, add the beef, stirring gently to separate, and 2 tsp Chinese yellow wine. Keep on stirring until the beef shreds are 'bouncing' in the pan.

雞
粥

DRY-FRIED FRENCH BEANS
Highly savoury pure
vegetable dishes — such
as this Sichuan specialty —
are often used as a
contrast to a pure meat
dish in the composition of
a well balanced meal.

**SHREDDED AUBERGINES IN
FISH-FLAVOUR SAUCE**
This full-flavoured and
somewhat spicy dish is
excellent with rice,
especially in the absence
of a substantial meat dish.

SICHUAN BRAISED BEAN CURD
This is a very well known
Sichuan dish which is now
extremely popular all over
China — and is also a
great favourite in Japan! It
should be served with
rice, either plain boiled
rice, or rice stir-fried with
egg.

七彩銀芽

Thoroughly mix together the seasonings and add them to the beef. Stir-fry over a high heat for 45 seconds. Add 1 tbsp sugar and 1 tsp Chinese yellow wine. Stir-fry for 15 seconds.

Add the celery and carrot, stir-fry for 30 seconds before adding the ginger, spring onion and peppercorn powder. Stir and serve.

The dry-frying method is an unique contribution to Chinese cuisine developed by Sichuan chefs. Beer, rather than mint, is the best accompaniment to this particular dish.

DRY-FRIED FRENCH BEANS

350g (12oz) French beans
1 dried red chilli
225ml (8floz/1 cup) peanut oil
1 tbsp chopped garlic
1 tsp chopped ginger
1 tbsp chopped dried shrimps

Seasoning
2 tsp rice wine

1 tsp monosodium glutamate
   (optional)
1/2 tsp salt
1 tsp sugar

2 tsp dark soy sauce
8 tbsp water
1/2 tsp sesame oil
1 tsp vinegar

Trim the beans and cut each one in half. Chop the chilli into small pieces.

Heat the pan until it is very hot. Add the peanut oil. Fry the French beans and remove after 30 seconds. Drain the oil away.

Heat 1 tbsp oil in pan, add the chopped garlic, ginger and dried shrimps and stir-fry until fragrant (about 30 seconds). Add the seasonings and French beans to the pan and sauté for a further 30 seconds.

Add the soy sauce and water and simmer over low heat until the sauce has almost evaporated.

Add the sesame oil and vinegar and sauté for a short while longer over high heat. Serve.

SHREDDED AUBERGINES IN FISH-FLAVOUR SAUCE

500g (1 1/4lb) aubergines
1 red chilli
1/2 stalk of celery
1 stalk of Chinese parsley
2 stalks of spring onions
450ml (16floz/2 cups) peanut oil
2 tsp chopped garlic
1 tsp chilli and bean paste
2 tsp rice wine lees or Chinese
   yellow wine

1 tsp chopped ginger
8 tbsp good stock

Seasoning
1/2tsp salt
1 tsp monosodium glutamate
   (optional)
1 1/2 tsp wine vinegar
2 tsp chilli sauce

Peel the aubergines and cut them into thin slices.

Cut the chilli, celery and Chinese parsley into 1cm (½in) slices and the spring onions into shavings.

Heat the pan until it is very hot. Add the oil and, when the oil begins to smoke, add the aubergines. Fry for 30 seconds. Remove the aubergines as soon as they start to turn brown and drain away the oil.

Heat the pan again until it is very hot and pour 2 tbsp oil into it. Add the chopped chilli, celery and Chinese parsley together with the chopped garlic, chilli and bean paste, rice wine and chopped ginger and stir-fry until fragrant. Add the stock and then the seasonings.

Put in the sliced aubergines and cook over high heat until most of the liquid is gone. Remove and place on a plate. Sprinkle with the chopped spring onions and serve.

This vegetable dish is delicious with plain cooked rice. 'Fish-flavour', a Sichuan speciality, is unique in Chinese cuisine. There are several explanations as to why it is so called (it certainly *doesn't* taste of fish!). The most convincing is that it was originally used for fish dishes.

SICHUAN BRAISED BEAN CURD

4 tbsp peanut oil	300g/11oz)
50g (2oz) minced beef	4 tbsp chicken stock
1 tbsp chilli broad bean paste	2 tsp cornflour, softened in 2 tsp
1 tsp chopped garlic	water
1 tsp chilli oil	1 tbsp chopped spring onion
½ tsp chilli powder	1½ tsp Sichuan peppercorn
2 tsp dark soy sauce	powder
4 cakes bean curd (approximately	2 tsp Chinese Yellow wine

Heat the oil in a pan, add the minced beef and chilli broad bean paste and cook for 30 seconds, stirring continuously. Add the chopped garlic, chilli oil, chilli powder and soy sauce, stir-fry and cook for 1 minute. Chop the bean curd into 1cm (½in) cubes and add to the pan together with the chicken stock, stirring and mixing all the time. When the contents boil, reduce the heat and simmer for 5 minutes.

Stir in the blended cornflour and add the chopped spring onion and peppercorn powder. Stir in the wine and serve.

This is perhaps the best known Sichuan dish outside the province, and extremely popular in overseas Chinese restaurants. It is excellent with rice or bread — whether Chinese steamed bread or a hard-crust French loaf.

EASTERN SCHOOL

CRABS FROM SHANGHAI are
sold at market tied with
sea grass.

(*Opposite page*) A
TRADITIONAL SHANGHAI
tea-house built on a lake.

Of all China's regional cuisines, that of Shanghai is the most diverse. Not surprisingly, for the region covers three major East China Sea coastal provinces — Kiangsu, Chekiang and Fukien — and the two inland provinces of Anhwei and Kiangsi. The southernmost of the coastal provinces, Fukien, has its own distinctive styles of cooking, its isolated communities having over a hundred different dialects and almost as many culinary peculiarities. In the Yangtze delta area, dominated by the city of Shanghai, many famous cities have contributed major dishes and techniques to what we broadly label Shanghai food.

Two geographical features ensured that the Shanghai region would be rich both economically and in culinary terms. First, the coastline, which extends from Fukien in the south through Chekiang Province, up to Kiangsu Province. Seafood in many forms is an eastern region joy. Second, the Yangtze, Asia's longest and China's most important commercial river, is a 3,400-mile lifeline. Networks of irrigation canals running from it increased the fertility of the Yangtze valley, as in Sichuan. In the river estuary itself is a cluster of famous cities — Suzhou, Hangzhou, Yangzhou, Nanking — as well as Shanghai itself. On the Yung River estuary south of Shanghai lies Ningpo, one of the original treaty ports.

First let us look at Shanghai, China's largest city. The independent municipality in south-east Kiangsu Province has 12 million inhabitants, who live in a city that is often compared with Hong Kong, for Shanghai was only a glorified fishing village until the middle of the nineteenth century. The Treaty of Nanking (1842) opened it and other coastal ports to foreign trade. The rest is history, as they say, but old Shanghai, the original community outside the Foreign Concessions, did have its own cuisine, and that native Shanghainese culinary tradition still defines the basic outlines of Shanghai food. Generally it is more greasy, sugary and strongly flavoured than food from other regions, and stewing, frying and braising are its principal cooking techniques. As usual, climatic considerations seem to have caused the characteristics.

Shanghai winters tend to be cold. As in northern China, bread, dumplings and noodles, particularly plump noodles, were favoured, as was oil. In contrast, the summers were warmer, usually uncomfortably hot. Soya bean products were the customary Chinese response to the human need for cooling food. Preserved foods were essential ingredients, preserved vegetables, fish, shrimps, mushrooms are Shanghainese specialities. The 100-day-old egg is a famed Shanghai favourite.

Any saltiness in the preserved ingredients was balanced by other flavourings, and sugar was a frequent additive to meat dishes (as in Korea). Perhaps understandably, native Shanghainese food has never been considered sophisticated enough to be served at elegant banquets, that honour having been reserved for Peking and Cantonese food.

In the nineteenth century, however, Shanghai became China's most cosmopolitan city. Pictures of the famed riverside Bund reveal the foreign architectural influences that overwhelmed the seaport, but they cannot show the various cultural and culinary influences, both from outside and also from within China, that created the Shanghainese love of good food and dining out.

The port of Ningpo, an older trading centre, gave the region's cuisine its saltiness. Salt and preserved ingredients are strongly featured in Ningpo dishes, and the steamed and fish dishes, which were also highly developed in Ningpo, contributed several renowned dishes to the Shanghai repertoire. Two examples are braised turtle in sweet brown sauce and yellow fish in soup.

Hangzhou is deservedly famous. During the later Sung dynasty it was the capital of south China and famed for its silk. Marco Polo thought it the 'finest and most splendid city in the world'. He wrote with mouth-watering approval of its 'abundance of victuals', its 'plump and tasty' lake fish, and its fresh, spiced rice wine. The West Lake of Hangzhou gave the ancient city fine, freshwater fish as well as natural beauty. Some of the fine results include West Lake vinegar fish, and West Lake watercress is a connoisseur's delight. The tea-houses by the lake were famed for their service of another Hangzhou speciality, Dragon Well Tea (*Loong Ching*). The tea is China's finest, a delicate, slightly bitter green tea, as rare and special as good champagne and still used for special state occasions.

Hangzhou has other claims to fame. Hangzhou dumplings are gloriously filled with meat and sauce. Quick-fried shredded eel, often regarded as a Shanghainese delicacy, actually originated in Hangzhou, as did the beggar's chicken, mentioned in the introduction to Peking cuisine, which happily adopted a Hangzhou peasant thief's invention!

OUTSIDE SHANGHAI, China's largest city, the scenery and way of life of the Yangtze delta remain unchanged.

Suzhou was another Sung dynasty city of grace and beauty. An old Chinese saying claimed that 'Above is paradise; here below are Suzhou and Hangzhou'. Another watery wonderland of bridges and streams, Suzhou attracted poets and gourmets.

Favourite Suzhou recipes are Chinese ham in honey sauce and winter bamboo shoots with shrimp eggs (salty preserved goodness reappearing in fine forms). Suzhou is also associated with the freshwater crabs, known to the world as Shanghai crabs. Every autumn the crabs emerge from the Yangtze River mudlands, their mating urges driving them on to dry land and into fishermen's traps. Millions of them find themselves trussed up in green grass thongs, packed in ice and shipped off as a major export from Shanghai.

Shaohsing wine, a product of the fertile river valley, is a rice spirit that appears in many Chinese dishes. Other products of the area include Zhenjiang's vinegar and Amoy's soy sauce.

One authority believes that some of China's best vegetarian dishes are found in the Shanghai school of cooking. Such dishes are made by both Taoist and Buddhist chefs: Buddhists do not eat meat from religious conviction while Taoists have long studied the correct use of vegetables for long life and good health.

Away from the monasteries other meat dishes were being pioneered in the Shanghai region. Thus Nanking, a former capital during troubled times, has given us fine pressed duck, and Wuxi exported the idea and brilliance of sweet-and-sour pork spare ribs. Sizzling rice dishes come from the eastern region, from Yangzhou, which was also the home of the banquet-ending rice and noodles with vegetables.

The cuisine of Fukien Province bears a closer relationship to the cooking traditions of its neighbours to the south, Chiu Chow and Guangzhou. Amoy and Fuzhou are the province's major ports, facing the Taiwan Strait, and in the past centuries, thousands of Fukienese emigrated from such ports to take their diverse culinary ideas to the Philippines, Singapore and elsewhere.

A SUMMER HOUSE on Hangzhou's West Lake.

One Shanghainese element in their cooking is the frequent use of the 'red cooking' technique, a slow stewing or braising of soy-sauced dishes, in which the reduction of cooking oils produces hot tastiness. Unless the dish is eaten quickly, the greasiness for which Shanghainese food is notorious emerges.

Generally meticulously chopped or shredded, Fukienese food is of a soft consistency and soups are favourites. Congee, which a westerner might call rice porridge, is a Fukienese speciality, but most of the province's dishes are plain and simple and many of them employ the southern technique of stir-frying.

With all the variety of Shanghainese cooking it's not surprising that a typical overseas Shanghainese café menu can be both massive and baffling. It will have Sichuan and Cantonese dishes, along with dishes favoured by the seagoing Hoklo or farming Hakka peoples. For Shanghai was a cultural melting pot for a century and also renowned for its 'Russian' bakeries. It was also a region of convivial, gregarious diners who did not stand on ceremony. They were snackers rather than banqueteers, for Shanghai was the city of business while Peking was the seat of government. Shanghai was exciting. It was a city for all seasons and its Shanghainese cooking proves it.

清炒蝦仁

STIR-FRIED SHRIMPS WITH GREEN PEAS

苑碗荳蝦仁

STIR-FRIED SHRIMPS WITH
GREEN PEAS
This dish can be prepared
almost in an instant by
stir-frying. Indeed, the
shortness of the cooking
time is a key factor in the
quality of the result: a
crisp outer shell with a
fresh, juicy morsel within.
Biting into the shrimp
should feel exactly like
biting into an apple.

STIR-FRIED BROAD BEANS,
SHRIMPS, HAM AND BUTTON
MUSHROOMS
In this semi-soup dish the
flavour of the beans is set
off against the savouriness
of the shrimps and the
richly flavoured sauce.

STIR-FRIED SHRIMPS WITH GREEN PEAS

500g (1¼lb) shrimps, shelled and
deveined

Marinade
1 egg white
2 tsp cornflour
1 tsp salt

1 tsp sesame oil
450ml (16floz/2 cups) peanut oil
2 slices ginger
250g (9oz) green peas
2 tbsp chicken stock
½ tsp salt
1 tsp Chinese yellow wine

Clean the shrimps and pat them dry. Mix together the marinade ingredients, add the shrimps and refrigerate for 30 minutes.

Heat 2 tbsp oil in a pan. Add the ginger but remove and discard it when it has browned. Add the green peas to the pan and the stock and ½ tsp salt. Cook for 2 minutes, remove, drain and set aside. Heat 450ml (16floz/2 cups) oil in the pan and add the shrimps, stirring to separate. Remove.

Reheat the pan, return the shrimps and green peas and add the Chinese yellow wine. Stir rapidly over a very high heat for 30 seconds and serve.

STIR-FRIED SHRIMPS

500g (1¼lb) shelled shrimps, fresh
or frozen
1 egg white
2 tsp cornflour
450ml (16floz/2 cups) peanut oil

Seasonings
1½ tsp chopped root ginger
2 tsp chopped spring onion
2 tsp Chinese yellow wine
few drops vinegar
1 tsp salt

Clean the shrimps and dry them with a paper towel. Blend the egg white and cornflour and coat the shrimps with the mixture.

Bring the oil to the boil. Add the shrimps, stirring to separate. After 30 seconds remove the shrimps from the pan quickly and drain them thoroughly.

Heat the pan until it is very hot and add 1 tbsp peanut oil. Add the seasonings and then the shrimps. Stir rapidly for 20 seconds over a high heat.

STIR-FRIED BROAD BEANS, SHRIMPS, HAM AND BUTTON MUSHROOMS

500g (1¼lb) broad beans

Marinade
½ egg white

1 tsp cornflour
1 tsp salt
¼ tsp sesame oil

苑
碗
荳
蝦
仁

250g (9oz) shrimps, shelled and
    deveined

100g (4oz) ham
100g (4oz) button mushrooms
225ml (8floz/1 cup) peanut oil

3-4 slices ginger
2 cloves garlic, crushed
225ml (8floz/1 cup) chicken stock
2 tsp Chinese yellow wine
2 tbsp cornflour
1 tsp sugar
1 tsp salt

Skin the beans and top-and-tail them. Set aside.

Prepare the marinade. Clean the shrimps, pat them dry and set them aside to marinate.

Cut the ham into 2mm ($\frac{1}{8}$in) thin slices, then cut it into 1cm ($\frac{1}{2}$in) squares. Set aside.

Cut the mushrooms horizontally in halves. Set aside.

Heat the oil. When it is hot add the shrimps, stirring to separate. After 30 seconds remove and drain. Set aside.

Fry the beans and button mushrooms in the oil for 1$\frac{1}{2}$ minutes over a high heat. Remove, drain and set aside.

Heat 3 tbsp oil in the pan. Add the ginger slices and crushed garlic and remove and discard them when browned.

Return the shrimps to the pan. Sauté for 30 seconds, stir and add the broad beans, ham and mushrooms. Add the remaining ingredients, stir and bring to the boil quickly. Continue to stir-fry over high heat for 1$\frac{1}{2}$ minutes and serve.

SHANGHAI QUICK-FRY SHRIMPS

350g (12oz) fresh shrimps, shelled
1 egg white
2 tsp cornflour
450ml (16floz/2 cups) peanut oil

Seasonings
1$\frac{1}{2}$ tsp chopped ginger

1$\frac{1}{2}$ tsp chopped spring onion
1$\frac{1}{2}$ tsp rice wine
2 drops white vinegar
1 tsp monosodium glutamate
    (optional)
$\frac{1}{2}$ tsp of salt

Clean the shrimps and dry them with a towel.

Mix together the egg white and cornflour and use the mixture to coat the shrimps.

Bring the oil to a high temperature in a pan.

Add the shrimps, stir to separate and fry for 15 seconds. Remove the shrimps from the pan with a perforated spoon and drain away the oil.

Heat a pan or wok until it is very hot. Pour 1 tbsp peanut oil into it and add the seasonings and the shrimps. Fry for 20 seconds over a high heat and serve.

The success of this dish relies very much on temperature — it needs very high heat and quick stir-frying.

清蒸河鰻

STEAMED EEL and
(*below*) SIZZLING EEL
Eel is a favourite dish all
along the Yangtze River.
In Shanghai, along the
lower reaches of this great
waterway, the eel flesh is
often steamed and
presented more delicately
than in Sichuan and the
upper Yangtze. There the
sauce used is much more
spicy: the eel is first fried,
then cut into strips to be
given a turn in a highly
spiced sauce (see picture
below). The Shanghai
version is excellent with
wine: the overpowering
flavour of the Sichuan
version is best with
quantities of rice.

炒蟮糊

WEST LAKE FISH
Most of the larger Chinese cities, including Shanghai, have a West Lake — a place where the townsfolk can relax and entertain themselves. The title of this dish denotes the proximity of the water in which the fish (usually carp) was caught — and thus the freshness of the fish. This is a deep-fry version which may be presented with either a savoury or sweet-and-sour sauce, the total flavour made more distinctive by sprinkling the dish with chopped coriander.

207

清蒸河鰻

STEAMED EEL

1kg (2lb) white eel
6 slices ginger
2 spring onions
8 tbsp peanut oil
1 tsp Chinese yellow wine

225ml (8floz/1 cup) chicken stock
1 tsp salt
1 tsp sugar
½ tsp pepper
1 tbsp cornflour

Put the eel in a basin and pour over it 2l (4 pints/10 cups) boiling water with 2 tbsp salt added. Wash the fish thoroughly. Slit the eel open, remove the intestines and clean the inside carefully. Pat it dry with paper towels.

Make deep cuts (about three-quarters of the way through the flesh) at 25mm (1in) intervals along the eel and place it on a plate, bending it into a ring form. Arrange the ginger and spring onion on top.

Steam the eel over a medium heat for 20 minutes. Remove the ginger and spring onions and discard them and drain away the liquid from the plate. Heat the oil and pour it over the eel, again draining any excess from the plate.

Add the remaining ingredients to the pan, stir and bring to the boil. Pour the sauce over the eel and serve.

SIZZLING EEL

1kg (2lb) yellow eels
2l (4 pints/10 cups) boiling water
2 tbsp salt
4 tbsp peanut oil
2 tsp chopped ginger
½ tsp pepper
2 tsp Chinese yellow wine
1 tbsp sugar

2 tbsp dark soy sauce
8 tbsp chicken stock
1½ tbsp cornflour dissolved in 1½
*   tbsp water*
2 tsp chopped spring onion
2 tbsp sesame oil
2 tsp minced ham
1½ tsp chopped coriander

Place the eels in a basin. Pour over them the boiling water (to which has been added 2 tbsp salt) and let them stand for 3 minutes. Take the eels out of the water and rinse them in cold water from the tap.

Separate the meat from the bone with the handle of a teaspoon, then cut the eel meat into 1 × 5cm (½ × 2in) strips. Set aside. Heat the oil until very hot. Add the eel, stirring, and add the chopped ginger, pepper, yellow wine, sugar, soy sauce and chicken stock. Cook for 5 minutes. Stir in the cornflour and transfer to a plate. Make a small well in the centre of the eels and put into it the chopped spring onion.

Heat 2 tbsp sesame oil until very hot and pour it into the 'well'. Add the minced ham, garnish with coriander and serve.

西
湖
醋
魚

WEST LAKE FISH

1kg (2lb) carp
2 tbsp shredded ginger
3 tbsp shredded spring onion
140ml (5fl oz/generous $\frac{1}{2}$ cup)
   peanut oil

Sauce
225ml (8fl oz/1 cup) chicken stock
1 tbsp sugar
1 tbsp brown vinegar
1 tsp salt
$\frac{1}{4}$ tsp pepper
$1\frac{1}{2}$ tbsp cornflour
2 tsp Chinese yellow wine

Put the fish in a basin. Pour over it 1l (2 pints) boiling water and leave it to stand for 1 minute.

Scrape off the scales and place the fish on a chopping-board. Slicing horizontally, cut the fish in two, one side with the back bone, the other without. On the side with the back bone, make five deep slits, approximately 3cm ($1\frac{1}{2}$in) apart.

On the meat side of the other half make a long lengthwise slit, but do not cut through the skin.

Place the whole fish, including the head, on a plate. Spread the ginger and half the spring onion over it and steam over a high heat for 10 minutes. Remove and discard the spring onion and arrange the remaining fresh spring onion on top of the fish. Heat 8 tbsp peanut oil and pour it over the fish, draining away any excess.

Heat 2 tbsp oil in a pan and add the sauce ingredients. Bring the sauce to the boil, pour it over the fish and serve.

CHICKEN 'SAUCE'

600g ($1\frac{1}{2}$lb) young chicken
2 tbsp lard
$1\frac{1}{2}$ tbsp rice wine or dry sherry
2 tbsp soy sauce
1 tbsp sugar

8 tbsp stock
1 tbsp cornflour
2 spring onions, cut into 25mm
   (1in) pieces

Cut off the wings and parson's nose from the chicken and chop it into about 20 pieces, with the bone still attached.

Heat the lard over a high heat; stir-fry the chicken pieces for about 30 seconds.

Add the wine or sherry, soy sauce and sugar, stir until the chicken turns brown, then add the stock. Bring to the boil, reduce the heat to simmer for 10 minutes or until the stock is reduced by a third.

Increase the heat, add the cornflour, mixed in a little water, and

醉
雞

DRUNKEN CHICKEN

Served principally as a
cold *hors d'oeuvre*, the
chicken is lightly boiled,
then immersed in wine for
a period which may be a
few hours or a few days.
The chicken used should
be a free-range fowl for
choice: if not, the chicken
should be marinated
overnight to improve its
flavour.

BEGGAR'S CHICKEN

This amusing barbecue
dish should be cooked for
several hours in the
embers of a hot fire. The
chicken, well marinated, is
wrapped in lotus leaves
than plastered with mud.
The name of the dish
indicates the Chinese
admiration for the
resourcefulness of the
poor man — and suggests
that the recipe should
begin 'First steal one
chicken'.

醬爆櫻桃

HONEY HAM
The Chinese often use honey, sugar or syrup to cook or flavour salty meat. This is a typical example, in which the saltiness of the ham contrasts interestingly with the sweetness of the honey sauce.

STIR-FRIED FROGS' LEGS IN BROWN SAUCE
In Chinese cuisine, frog is treated like chicken, with the advantage that frog can be cooked in even less time than chicken. This is really a reproduction chicken dish in which the frog is cooked very quickly in a brown soya-paste sauce. The fresh savouriness of the frog is contrasted with the earthier savour of the brown sauce: the dish can be made more aromatic by the last-minute addition of some wine.

blend well. When the juice is further reduced by half, add the onions and serve.

Each chicken piece should be coated in a dark, thick sauce, hence the name of this dish.

DRUNKEN CHICKEN

1kg (2lb) chicken	100g (4oz) ginger
1 tbsp salt	225ml (8fl oz/1 cup) Chinese
2 spring onions	yellow wine

Clean the chicken thoroughly. Bring 2l (4 pints) water to the boil, turn off the heat, place the chicken in the hot water and turn it over. Poach the chicken for 1 minute, remove, drain and pat it dry with an absorbent paper towel.

Rub ½ tbsp salt over the skin and spoon ½ tbsp salt into the cavity. Finely shred the spring onion and ginger and stuff them into the cavity. Finally, pour the Chinese yellow wine into the cavity.

Steam the chicken over medium heat for 20 minutes in a shallow basin. Remove it and chop it into bite-size pieces. Return the chicken pieces to the wine in the basin, soak overnight and transfer to a plate to serve.

HONEY HAM

350g (12oz) Chinese ham	2 tbsp peanut oil
300g (11oz) candied lotus seeds	1 tsp dried laurel blossoms
120g (4½oz) sugar	(cointreau is a good substitute)

Clean the ham thoroughly with hot water before placing it in a deep container. Add sufficient water to cover and steam for 2 hours. Remove and drain.

Place the candied lotus seeds in a separate container and add 225ml (8fl oz/1 cup) water. Steam for 2 hours and set aside.

Cut the ham into slices 25 × 60 × 2mm (1 × 2½ × ⅛in) and arrange them neatly in a medium-size bowl. Add water to cover the ham and steam for 30 minutes. Drain, sprinkle with sugar and steam for another 30 minutes.

Arrange the ham slices carefully on top of the lotus seeds and steam for 10 minutes.

Heat 2 tbsp oil in a pan and add the gravy from the ham. Add the dried laurel blossoms, stirring over a low heat for 1 minute. Pour the sweet gravy over the ham and serve.

STIR-FRIED FROGS' LEGS IN BROWN SAUCE

3 tbsp peanut oil	*1 tsp sugar*
6 spring onions (white part only)	*1 tbsp dark soy sauce*
2 tsp choppd ginger	*4 tbsp chicken stock*
24 pieces frogs' legs	*½ tsp five-spice powder*
1 tbsp Chinese yellow wine	*1 tsp sesame oil*

Heat 3 tbsp oil in a pan. Add the spring onions and ginger and when the aroma arises, add the frogs' legs. Stirring, cook over a very high heat for 30 seconds.

Add the yellow wine, sugar, dark soy sauce and chicken stock and, when they boil, reduce the heat and cook until the sauce has almost evaporated.

Sprinkle with five-spice powder and sesame oil, stir and serve.

BEGGAR'S CHICKEN

Marinade	*500g (1¼lb) pork*
2 tbsp dark soy sauce	*100g (4oz) Sichuan preserved*
4 tbsp Chinese yellow wine	*vegetables*
1 tsp sesame oil	*400g (14oz) bamboo shoots*
1 tsp sugar	*2 tbsp peanut oil*
1 tbsp salt	
	1 large piece suet
1½-2kg (3-4lb) chicken	*2 pieces lotus leaf*
	500g (1¼lb) wheat flour
Stuffing	*450ml (16floz/2 cups) water*
4-6 Chinese black mushrooms	*1 large piece foil*

Blend together the ingredients for the marinade and use three-quarters of the mixture to rub over the inside and outside of the chicken. Set aside.

Prepare the stuffing by soaking the black mushrooms in hot water for 30 minutes. Discard the stems and shred the caps.

Shred the pork and mix it with the remaining quarter of the marinade.

Shred the Sichuan preserved vegetables into matchstick-size pieces and soak them in water.

Shred the bamboo shoots into similar pieces and blanch them in boiling water for 2 minutes. (When using tinned bamboo shoots this is not necessary.)

Heat a pan, add 2 tbsp peanut oil and stir-fry the pork for 1 minute.

Add the shredded black mushrooms, bamboo shoots and Sichuan preserved vegetables. Cook for 30 seconds and stuff the

韭
黄
炒
肉
絲

**DRY-BRAISED BAMBOO SHOOTS
WITH PRESERVED SNOW
CABBAGE**
This is a dish for the
connoisseur because the
flavour of the fresh
bamboo shoot is
extremely subtle. Here it
is set off by a typical east
Chinese pickle which is
extremely salty. The dish
is often served as a hot
hors d'oeuvre for diners
to nibble at while they sip
their wine.

**STIR-FRIED SHREDDED PORK
AND CHINESE WHITE CHIVES**
This may be readily
produced in a very short
time, either as a hot *hors
d'oeuvre* to accompany
wine or to be added to
rice to increase the
savouriness of the whole
meal. Chinese chives are
not widely available but
are worth searching for.

**STIR-FRIED SHREDDED BEEF
AND GREEN PEPPER**
A lower Yangtze dish
which approximates to a
Sichuan (upper Yangtze)
dish of rather similar
composition. In the
version illustrated here,
chilli pepper has been
added to the stir-fry along
with the sweet pepper,
lending a spicy
savouriness to the dish.
Delicious with rice.

青椒牛肉絲

mixture generously into the cavity of the chicken.

Wrap the chicken in the piece of suet, trimming away any excess fat, and wrap the suet and chicken parcel in lotus leaves. (If you are using dried lotus leaves, soak them in hot water for 10 minutes first.)

Mix the flour and water and roll it out into a sheet. Encase the chicken parcel in the dough and wrap it all with foil.

Cook in a pre-heated oven at 230°C (450°F/Gas Mark 8) for 1 hour. Reduce the temperature to 180°C (350°F/Gas Mark 4) and bake for a further 45 minutes.

Remove the foil and crack the casing with a pestle. Remove the lotus leaves and transfer the chicken to a serving platter.

STIR-FRIED SHREDDED BEEF AND GREEN PEPPER

300g (11oz) fillet of beef	*1 egg white*
Marinade	*500g (1¼lb) green pepper*
1 tbsp light soy sauce	*225ml (8floz/1 cup) peanut oil*
1 tsp dark soy sauce	*1 tsp salt*
1 tsp sugar	*2 tsp chopped ginger*
1 tbsp cornflour	*2 tsp choppd garlic*
2 tbsp Chinese yellow wine	*2 tsp Chinese yellow wine*

Shred the beef and mix the pieces thoroughly with the marinade mixture in a bowl. Allow to stand for 15 minutes.

Shred the green pepper.

Heat the oil in a pan and add the beef, stirring to separate the shreds. Remove after 75 seconds, drain and set aside.

Heat 1 tbsp oil in the pan, add the green pepper and 1 tsp of salt, stir-frying for 2 minutes over high heat. Remove and set aside.

Heat 2 tbsp oil in the pan. Add the ginger and garlic and, when the aroma arises, return the beef and green pepper to the pan. Add any of the marinade mixture that is left in the bowl and stir-fry over very high heat for 2½ minutes. Add Chinese yellow wine and serve.

STIR-FRIED SHREDDED PORK AND CHINESE WHITE CHIVES

500g (1¼lb) fillet of pork	*1 egg white*
	1 tbsp cornflour
Marinade	*2 tsp Chinese yellow wine or dry*
1 tbsp light soy sauce	*sherry*
½ tsp sesame oil	

韭黄炒肉絲

2 medium black mushrooms
250g (9oz) Chinese white chives or
    young leeks
225ml (8fl oz/1 cups) peanut oil
1½ tsp chopped ginger

1 tsp chopped garlic
1 tsp salt
1 tsp Chinese yellow wine or dry
    sherry

Cut the fillet of pork into 2mm (⅛in) thin slices. Then into 5cm (2in) shreds. Mix the pieces of meat with the marinade and set aside for 15 minutes.

Soak the black mushrooms in hot water for 30 minutes. Remove and discard the stems and cup the caps into fine shreds. Cut the chives or leeks into shreds 5cm (2in) long.

Heat 225ml (8fl oz/1 cup) peanut oil in pan. Add the pork, stirring to separate, reduce the heat, and leave to sit in the oil for 2 minutes. Remove, drain and set aside.

Heat 2 tbsp oil in a pan. Add the ginger and garlic, return the pork and add the mushrooms, chives or leeks and salt. Stir and cook over high heat for 2 minutes, add the Chinese yellow wine, stir again and serve.

DRY-BRAISED BAMBOO SHOOTS WITH PRESERVED SNOW CABBAGE

250g (9oz) bamboo shoot
200g (7oz) preserved snow
    cabbage
4-6 stalks spring onion (white part
    only)
4 tbsp peanut oil

3-4 slices ginger
1 tsp salt
1 tbsp sugar
2 tbsp Chinese yellow wine
4 tbsp chicken stock

Cut the bamboo shoot into wedges 2cm (¾in) long.

Soak the preserved snow cabbage in 1l (2 pints) cold water for 30 minutes. Change the water and soak for a further 15 minutes. Drain the snow cabbage and chop it into sections 3cm (1½in) long. Then cut the spring onion into sections the same length.

Heat 2 tbsp oil in a pan and add the spring onions and ginger. When the aroma arises, add the bamboo shoot and snow cabbage and stir-fry over a high heat for 2 minutes.

Add the remaining ingredients and continue to stir-fry and cook over a very high heat for 3 minutes. Remove from the heat and drain away any remaining liquid.

Heat 2 tbsp oil in the pan until very hot. Return the drained bamboo shoot and snow cabbage to fry for a further 2 minutes. Remove and drain again on a paper towel before transferring to the serving dish.

GLOSSARY

Bamboo shoots: There are several kinds of bamboo shoots available in the west — all in tins only, which is a pity since they lose much of their crispy texture and flavour. Try to obtain *Winter bamboo shoots*; they are dug up from the cracked earth before the shoots grow to any great length or size and are therefore extra tender and tasty. Spring bamboo shoots are much larger; they sometimes may reach several feet in length and 7-10cm (3-4in) in diameter. Once the tin is opened, the shoots may be kept in a covered jar of water in the refrigerator for several days. *Braised bamboo shoots* in tins should be eaten cold without any further cooking.

Bean curd (tofu): Made from soaked yellow soy beans ground with water. A coagulant is added after some of the water is strained through muslin cloth, causing the ground beans to curdle and become firm bean curd. Usually sold in squares about 6×6cm (2½×2½in) and 2cm (¾in) thick, it will keep a few days if submerged in water in a container and placed in the coldest part of a refrigerator. *Dried bean curd skin* is usually sold either in thick sticks or thin sheets. It should be soaked in cold water overnight or in warm water for at least an hour before use.

Bean sauce: Sometimes called 'Crushed bean sauce', this thick sauce is made from black or yellow beans, flour and salt. It is sold in tins and, once opened, must be transferred into a screw-top jar and then it will keep in a refrigerator for months. (N.B. Black bean sauce is very salty, while yellow bean sauce is sweeter with sugar added.)

Bean sprouts: Two kinds are available: *yellow soy bean sprouts*, only to be found in Chinese provision stores, and *green mung bean sprouts*, which can be bought from almost every large city supermarket. (Never use tinned bean sprouts, they do not have the crunchy texture which is the main characteristic of bean sprouts.) They can be kept in the refrigerator for two or three days if bought fresh.

Cellophane or transparent noodles: Made from mung beans. They are sold in dried form, tied into bundles weighing from 50g (2oz) to 450kg (1lb). Soak in warm water for 5 minutes before use.

Chilli paste: Also called 'Chilli purée'. Is made of chilli, soy bean, salt, sugar and flour. Sold in jars, it will keep almost indefinitely.

Chilli sauce: Hot, red sauce made from chillies, vinegar, plums, salt and sesame.

Chinese cabbage: There are innumerable varieties of cabbage grown in China, of which only two or three types are available in the west. The one most commonly seen is known as celery cabbage or Chinese leaves (*Brassica pekinensis*), it has a pale green colour and tightly wrapped elongated head; two-thirds of the vegetable is stem which has a crunchy texture. Another variety has a shorter and fatter head with curlier, pale yellow leaves. Then there is the dark green-leaved variety, also with white stems (*Brassica chinensis*), and the bright green-leaved variety with pale green stems, sometimes with a sprig of yellow flower in the centre (*Brassica parachinensis*) which is very much prized by the Chinese. These last two varieties are sold only in Chinese stores.

Chinese dried mushrooms: There are two main types of Chinese mushrooms: those that grow on trees, known as Black or Winter Mushrooms (*Lentinus edodes*); and those cultivated on a bed of straw, known as Straw Mushrooms (*Volvariella volvacea*). Black or Winter Mushrooms are sold dried; they are used in many dishes as a complementary vegetable for their flavour and aroma. Soak in warm water for 20-30 minutes, squeeze dry and discard the hard stalks before use. Straw Mushrooms are available in tins and are completely different in texture and flavour. The western varieties of common or field mushrooms (*Agaricus bisporus* or *Psalliota campestris*) can be used as substitutes.

Five-spice powder: A mixture of anise seed, fennel, cloves, cinnamon and pepper. It is very strongly piquant, so use a very small amount each time. It will keep for years if stored in a tightly covered container.

Fresh coriander: Sometimes known as Chinese parsley, this plant is available in oriental stores, or in Italian grocers where it is called *cilantro*.

Ginger root: Sold by weight. Should be peeled and sliced or finely chopped before use. Will keep for weeks in a dry, cool place. Dried and powdered ginger is not a satisfactory substitute for fresh ginger.

Green hot chilli: Will keep fresh for a week or two in the vegetable compartment of the refrigerator in a plastic bag.

Hoisin sauce: Also known as barbecue sauce. Made from soy beans, sugar, flour, vinegar, salt, garlic, chilli and sesame.

You will have noticed that I have not listed **monosodium glutamate** (MSG). This chemical compound, sometimes known as 'taste essence' (*veh t'sin*), is often used to heighten the flavour of food. It is rather frowned upon by true gourmets as it can wipe out the subtle flavours of a dish when used to excess, so use with discretion.

Oyster sauce: A thick sauce made from oysters and soy sauce. Sold in bottles, it will keep in the refrigerator indefinitely.

Red bean curd sauce: A thick sauce made from fermented bean curd and salt. Sold in tins or jars, it will keep indefinitely.

Rice wine: Also known as Shaohsing wine, made from glutinous rice. Saké or pale (medium or dry) sherry can be substituted.

Salted black beans: Whole bean sauce, very salty.

Scallions: Also known as spring onions.

Sesame seed oil: Sold in bottles. Widely used in China as a garnish rather than for cooking. The refined yellow sesame oil sold in Middle Eastern stores has less flavour and therefore is not a very satisfactory substitute.

A few words must be said here regarding the types of oil used in Chinese cooking. The most commonly used in China are vegetable oils such as soy bean, peanut or rape seed oils. The Chinese never use butter or meat dripping, although lard and chicken fat are used in some regional cooking, notably in the Eastern School.

Sichuan preserved vegetable: This is a speciality of Sichuan province. It is the root of a special variety of the mustard green, pickled in salt and hot chilli. Sold in tins. Once opened it can be stored in a tightly sealed jar in the refrigerator for months.

Sichuan peppercorns: Reddish-brown peppercorns, much stronger than either black or white peppercorns of the west. Usually sold in plastic bags. Will keep indefinitely in a tightly sealed container.

Soy sauce: Sold in bottles or tins, this liquid sauce ranges from light to dark brown in colour. The darker coloured sauces are strongest and more often used in cooking, whereas the lighter are used at the table.

Tiger lily or **golden needles:** The buds of a special type of lily (*Hemerocallis fulva*). Sold in dried form, they should be soaked in warm water for 10-20 minutes and the hard stems removed. They are often used in combination with *Wood-ears.*

Tomato sauce: Quite different from western tomato ketchup. Italian tomato paste (purée) may be substituted when fresh tomatoes are not available.

Water chestnuts: Strictly speaking, water chestnuts do not belong to the chestnut family, they are the roots of a vegetable (*Heleocharis tuberosa*). Also known as *horse's hooves* in China on account of their appearance before the skin is peeled off, they are available fresh or in tins. Tinned water chestnuts retain only part of the texture, and even less of the flavour, of fresh ones. Will keep for about a month in a refrigerator in a covered jar.

Water chestnut powder: A flour made from water chestnuts. Cornflour is a good substitute.

Wood-ears: Also known as *Cloud Ears*, they are dried tree fungus (*Auricularia auricula*). Sold in dried form, they should be soaked in warm water for 20 minutes; discard any hard stems and rinse in fresh water before use. They have a crunchy texture and a mild but subtle flavour. According to the Chinese, Wood-ears contain protein, calcium, phosphorus, iron and carbohydrates, and one particular brand from Hupei Province claims on the packet (in English) that it 'possesses such effect as cleaning gastroenteric (sic!) organs in human body'.

INDEX

Page numbers in *italic* refer
to the illustrations.

223